SPEAK UP!

THE ULTIMATE GUIDE TO DOMINATE IN THE SPEAKING INDUSTRY

A Compilation by the Black Speakers Network

CONTENTS

FOREWORD BY DR. GEORGE C. FRASER

You can change someone's life by speaking and speaking can also change YOUR life. As sure as I am black, I know speaking changed by life.

Public speaking is no joke. I remember my first speaking event. It was a fiasco. I was a young executive at Procter & Gamble, three years into my career at the corporation. I was asked to deliver a presentation to about one hundred of my colleagues, clients, buyers, and corporate managers. I was excellent at one-on-one presentations – so how hard would it be to deliver a speech to 99 more?

Ha, was I wrong! The night before my boss asked me if I wanted to rehearse with him. I declined. I thought, "I got this." But when the day came, I choked and I nearly fainted.

Instead of delivering a speech, I was speechless. My boss, who knew me well and saw the signs, walked briskly but elegantly up to me, grabbed me by the shoulders and said, "George, you must be suffering from the effects of that flu bug we discussed last night."

Whew. I was like a limp rag and he escorted me from the room and sat me down. He helped me calm down and catch my breath.

Defeated, sitting outside the room where I expected to shine and dazzle, I was ready to give up on ever speaking before a group again, no matter how small. But I knew my failure was temporary and I would get up, mine the lessons I learned and get back on the horse — back in the speaking saddle... and the rest is history.

I became the first and only professional speaker in the world with five speeches published in the prestigious Vital Speeches of the Day Magazine (The Best Thought of the Best Minds On Current National Questions). In 2014, I was selected by several publications as One of The Best Speakers in America for style and content... content is king. Talking loudly and saying nothing will quickly sink your speaking career!

Bottom line... It is not how you start, it is how you finish. So, stay the course!

This book is the wisdom I wish I had when I started speaking. Here you have 32 experts telling you the ins and outs of the industry. If you read and heed these lessons, you will spare yourself a lot of grief and embarrassment. This is like having a personal mentor in your back pocket.

Read this book, then write your own! It will add demonstrated expertise and credibility to your words, ideas, and commitment to the art and science of speaking up.

Speak Up! The Ultimate Guide to Dominate in the Speaking Industry, a collaborative project by Black Speakers Network, is a tool to help you reach the next level in the speaking business.

www.frasernet.com

INTRODUCTION

Every day all around the world professionals and entrepreneurs from every industry do something that many people fear more than death. They take one last sip of water, stand up, walk to the front of a room, and speak up. Some people speak to win new business or to sell an idea. Some speak to share knowledge or transfer skills. While others, simply speak with the goal to uplift and inspire. Regardless, of why they speak, the goals for every speaker is the same - to use the spoken word as a catalyst for some sort of change.

Speaking can change your life. People who make the decision to Speak Up tend to experience more control over their career path, unlock new opportunities, and if desired, tap into completely new streams of income. Professional speaking is a billion-dollar industry, and while not every person has a desire to be a full-time professional speaker, the concepts, resources, and strategies presented in this book will position you to carve out your piece of the pie. If you are a current or aspiring professional speaker, consider this book your speaking 101 guide to understanding and navigating the basics of building a speaking business. Wherever you are on your journey, if speaking has been a life-long calling or a newly kindled interest *"Speak Up! The Ultimate Guide to Dominate in the Speaking Industry"* is here to serve as your road map to the next level.

There are many paths to success in the professional speaking industry. To help speakers cut through the confusion, Black Speakers Network created the 5M Model for Professional

Speaking ™ which is designed to help speakers develop the most essential knowledge and skills needed to build a profitable speaking business. These include.

- **Mission** - Gain clarity and uncover your authentic passion and purpose as a speaker

- **Message** - Learn what type of speaker you are and refine your core presentation skills

- **Marketing** - Develop strategies to reach and engage your target audience

- **Monetize** - Generate multiple streams of revenue for your speaking business

- **Management** - Create systems and processes to manage and grow your speaking business

Readers of this book will gain access to the expertise and wisdom of 32 remarkable co-authors who are current and emerging thought leaders, entrepreneurs, and expert speakers dedicated to advancing the mission of Black Speakers Network. In addition, you will find contributions from two titans in the speaking industry, Dr. George C. Fraser and Les Brown, who have both invested their lives in educating, empowering, and uplifting men and women particularly from underserved populations.

Mission!

This section will help you to gain clarity and uncover your authentic passion and purpose as a speaker

SPEAKING TO EVERYONE MEANS SPEAKING TO NO ONE!

FINDING AND SELECTING THE RIGHT SPEAKING OPPORTUNITIES

SUMMER ALEXANDER

There is only one audience you want to speak to and that is the audience who is most likely to take a predetermined, specific action once your speech concludes. Therefore, the first question you should ask before searching for speaking opportunities is - *What specific action do I want my audience to take at the end of my talk?*

If you are an author, perhaps you want them to purchase your book at the back of the room. If you are a consultant, you may want participants to visit your website and schedule a consultation. If you are speaking to educate, entertain, or motivate you will want an audience filled with engaged action takers.

Your presentation, your speaking style, and your call to action should be appropriate and relevant for your audience. Your job as a speaker is to gain an in-depth understanding of your ideal target audience. Having this understanding will help you to know what to say, how to say it, and where to find them. Your message, your product, your service, and/or your book are not going to resonate with everyone. It can be tempting to give a presentation that appeals to a broad audience, but your expertise will stand out more if you are a specialist instead of a generalist.

Once you are clear on who your audience is and what action you want them to take at the conclusion of your talk, your job then becomes to identify the organizations who are most likely to attract that audience to their events.

As you begin your search for speaking engagements, there are three key questions that you must answer for each organization you approach.

Does this organization align with my (personal and/or company) brand, message, vision, and core values?

Will this organization attract the audience who will be most impacted by my presentation?

Is the audience this organization will attract likely to take my desired action at the end of the presentation?

Additionally, you should reflect on the following questions as it relates to your qualifications as a speaker.

Do I have the knowledge, skills, and expertise to deliver a meaningful presentation to this audience?

Am I able to confidently share my message with this audience?

Do I have professional materials to properly market myself as a speaker?

One of the best ways to secure a speaking engagement is to give a dynamic presentation and ask for a referral from the speaker coordinator. Your next speaking engagement can easily come from a repeat invitation, from a referral, or from an audience member at your last engagement.

If you have never given a talk, consider starting small to get practice and feedback in order to solidify your presentation. Additionally, as you start your search it is important that you have a professional phone, email, and in-person pitch. Your approach when on the phone should be quick and to the point whereas with email or in person you have a little more opportunity to build rapport. You will also want to have professionally designed speaker marketing materials including a one sheet, headshot, and website.

Once you are ready to begin your search there are several ways both online and offline to identify potential speaking engagements.

Online Search

- **Utilize search terms**. Start with searching locally, statewide, nationwide, and lastly internationally. Visit Google and enter search terms that are relevant to your industry. If you are a social media expert, you would use search terms such as "call for social media speakers," "social media speaker submission," "social media speaker proposal" or "social media speaker application."

- **Find events.** Look for conferences, meetings, and events that are specific to your industry. If you are a leadership expert, you might be looking for events where there will be executives and managers in attendance. In this case, your search terms would include "executive leadership conference," "management conference," or "CEO conferences." You can also further narrow your search depending on your area of expertise with search terms such as "tech leadership conference" or "engineering leadership conference."

- **Search social media.** Utilize various social media platforms including but not limited to LinkedIn, Twitter, Facebook, and Instagram. Search using #hashtags to identify conferences in your industry and to identify other speakers in your industry who may leave clues to events where they have recently spoken. Some sample hashtags are #conference, #professionalspeaker, #speakerlife, #publicspeaker, and #keynotespeaker. Again, you can and should narrow the focus of your search by industry where appropriate.

- **Explore event platforms.** Sites such as Eventbrite.com, Meetup.com, Eventful.com, and Techevents.co are filled with events nationwide where there may be opportunities to speak. You should also check the websites of local convention bureaus and industry associations for upcoming events.

Offline Search

When seeking speaking opportunities, it is important that you do not limit your search to what you can find online. There are several offline strategies that can help you stand out and make meaningful connections with meeting planners and organization leaders.

- **Tap your personal network.** If there is an organization where you want to speak, scan your social media contacts, and check with friends, family, and current or former colleagues to see if you know anyone who works there. Send a copy of your speaker one sheet to your contacts and let them know you are currently booking speaking engagements and looking for introductions or referrals. Contact an organization where you have spoken in the past to let them know about any updates to your speaking topics and to find out if they would be interested in booking you to speak again.

- **Attend networking events.** Look for local networking events where they allow attendees to give a short elevator pitch and regularly invite guest speakers to present. If you have an opportunity to give a short pitch begin by giving some brief information about your background and professional expertise and be sure to mention that you are a speaker. Introduce yourself to leaders within the organization and inquire about any upcoming opportunities to speak.

- **Register for conferences.** Attend conferences and events to gain an understanding of the type of speakers they hire and to determine if your talk would be a good addition to their future lineup. Be sure to network with the speakers as well as the conference coordinators. Ask for contact information for any of the key players and follow up with them to learn when they will be accepting speaker proposals in the future.

If your search efforts are moving slower than you would like, do not be afraid to self-host an event to gain some momentum. For a relatively small cost, you can rent out a room in a local community center or library and host a small workshop. You can also host a webinar online where attendees can participate in your training from anywhere in the world from the comfort of their homes.

Key Takeaways

1. Prior to searching for speaking engagements make sure you are clear on what action you want your audience to take and what audience is most likely to take that action.

2. Look for speaking engagements that are a good match for your current speaking level, style, expertise, and background.

3. Utilize a combination of online and offline strategies to identify potential opportunities to speak.

4. Searching for speaking engagements is all about your numbers. You need to determine how many proposals you need to submit in order to secure one speaking engagement. From there you can set aside time in your monthly marketing activities to look for opportunities to submit proposals.

5. Rejection of your proposal is not a rejection of you! If you are submitting proposals but not securing speaking engagements, have a professional review your pitch and marketing materials to identify areas of improvement.

SUMMER ALEXANDER

 With a background in market research, technology, and communications; Summer Alexander is uniquely qualified to help businesses learn to combine the customer experience with their company data to create client-centered branding, messaging, and content strategy. As CEO of Simply Marketing Solutions, she leads the marketing strategy consulting firm and has advised clients in the areas of market analysis and industry research, content development and implementation, brand messaging, community outreach and social media strategy.

Summer is also a professional speaker and regularly conducts branding and marketing keynote presentations, staff trainings, and business workshops for governments, corporations, and non-profit organizations. Summer has been a featured speaker at events such as SXSW, The Chicago Women's Conference, and The Black Women's Expo among many others. She authored the Amazon #1 bestseller The Little Book of Big Marketing Ideas and is a co-author of The Power and Profit in Partnership. A recognized thought leader in her industry, Summer has been a featured guest expert in Black Enterprise, Jet, WGN TV, WCIU TV, Rolling Out Magazine and several other media outlets.

www.simplymarketingsolutions.com
www.linkedin.com/in/summeralexander

CLASS IS IN SESSION!

HOW TO GET BOOKED AS A COLLEGE SPEAKER

LINNITA HOSTEN

Two interesting facts about the college market:

1. It is an underserved audience in need of development.
2. Colleges/Universities have programming budgets to hire speakers.

This sounds like an ideal market that would be EASY to sell to, right? At least, I thought so when I started in 2013.

It was not until 2016, that I was able to break into the college market as an unpaid speaker. Then, two years later, after writing a book for the college audience - I entered the market as a paid speaker.

Here's a highlight of my insight on how to get booked as a college speaker:

Research

Get in the trenches about the college experience. Become knowledgeable about current issues and campus trends. Read case studies. Research movements and how campuses are responding to them (Me Too, gun laws, racial inequality, etc.)

The more aware you are of current trends, the more empowered and positioned you will be to create relevant and buyable programs for colleges.

The goal is to position yourself as a voice of authority in your niche by demonstrating a level of proficiency beyond personal storytelling and historic anecdotes. Speakers who have been able to endure long-term success in the college market, have developed a beyond surface-level understanding of their topics and have introduced "new thoughts" or "new perspectives" to the conversation.

Advice given to me when researching:

- Read the top books related to your niche
- Be familiar with the latest research related to your area of expertise
- Stay abreast of global news related to your audience
- Read academia publications that study your niche
- Absorb the information learned and find a unique way to teach the topic using your insight of research findings

Messaging

Only speakers who are able to creatively sell their programming actually breakthrough in the college market. This is why knowing your audience and their needs are so important. Your programming must be presented in a way that provides a solution to a current/common issue or trending topic. What will students walk away learning as a result of your programming? Why is your programming important to the college market?

After answering those questions, get creative and explore presenting your programming in a fun and convincing way. Some speakers utilize metaphors, acronyms, personal stories, etc.

Be prepared to also address why you are qualified to conduct your programming. Most speakers will capitalize on their personal experience. However, the best leverage is to capitalize on how your work has previously impacted other groups. This can include: Who applied your teachings and were positively impacted? Which organizations have endorsed your work? Which programs return for repeat business?

When you can succinctly answer these questions, you are on your way to effectively communicating your value proposition to prospective decision-makers and potential clients.

After you have developed your messaging and its unique value proposition, you can begin to solicit for speaking engagements. If you are able to convey your qualifications to speak in the college market (contrary to popular belief), you do not need experience with addressing the group. However, if you have an established authority (media exposure, speaking reel, products for the college audience, past college clients, etc.) you will have an advantage.

Submit Call for Speaker Proposals

This is the most critical stage of breaking into the college market. Your proposal submission not only needs to be catchy, relevant, and original; the proposal also needs to fit the theme of the event AND the audience.

The common mistake made by speakers when submitting their proposals is the same mistake job seekers make with their resume - not tailoring documents to fit the organization or role.

Refer to *#CallForSpeakers - How To Make Your Speaker Proposal Stand Out* for specific support with your proposal. However, if you can succinctly and creatively complete the form below, you are ready to submit:

Workshop Abstract:
A catchy summary of the workshop content typically limited to 150-200 words. Evaluators will ask among themselves "Would students find this interesting enough to attend. Is it relevant to today's student issues?"

Presenter Expertise & Qualifications:
Demonstration of qualification, experience, and expertise. What have you done or what are you doing that substantiates your credibility in this space?

Program Description:
Concise content details identifying the objectives of the program and summarizing the activities of the presentation.

Speak Up!

Additional Advice When Submitting Proposals:

- Review the conference booklet from the previous year and take note of how past presenters structured and marketed their keynote/workshop.

- Ask a Campus Activities professional or college student leader to review your proposal for college-audience relevance and creativity.

- Begin the proposal at least 15 days in advance of the submission deadline to ensure adequate time to think through ideas, test the idea with others and revise descriptions.

- Submit the proposal before it is due. Some evaluations factor in the timeliness of the submission.

- Never submit the same proposal twice (even if the proposal was accepted the previous year.) Event planners are looking for new and/or evolving content.

While Waiting to Hear Back

After submitting your program proposal, there will be a four to six week waiting period before you will receive a response. Use this time to position your media platforms as the ideal speaker. Blog once a week. Update your podcast. Engage on Twitter more frequently. Upload more IG content that supports and empowers your audience.

Many proposal applications will request your social media handle and web address. Expect evaluators to visit you online to see:

- The content you produce related to your topic
- Past events you have done with a similar audience
- The organizations that have endorsed your work

It is critical that if you do not have much or any past experience with this audience, that you are at least producing original content online.

If You Are Not Accepted

Expect to hear from the conference planning team within their designated timeline, if you do not receive an update, follow up.

If you are not accepted into a conference, try your best to acquire feedback on your proposal by asking the following questions:

- Could you share how I could improve my submission?
- Could you briefly discuss the factors that eliminated my proposal?
- What elements of my proposal could I improve to create a stronger submission?

If You Are Accepted

Congratulations! Now, get your creative wheels turning on how you will maximize the opportunity. Many college conferences do not compensate speakers who are selected by way of a call for proposals. However, large conferences will position you in a room of your target audience and potential buyers. This positioning is invaluable for all speakers in every stage of business and can allow you to:

- Build credibility and increase visibility with your target market

- Enter potential buyers in a sales funnel/email marketing campaign

- Collect email addresses to pitch upcoming events, programs, and/or related opportunities

- Pitch a series or component to your teaching such as a Facebook group, workbook, etc.

- & more

Outside of the Conference Method

Submitting proposals for large college conferences is one method to enter the market. Another method that may be a little more labor intensive is to submit your press kit and a brief email pitch to individual colleges or warm campus contacts.

By utilizing college websites (or LinkedIn), collect the contact information of campus activities staff, student leaders and/or student group advisors. Once the information is collected, develop an email pitch, and send out correspondences. Be sure to create a spreadsheet to track the correspondences and/or to note any comments or feedback.

Additional Advice

- Keep the initial email communication brief

- Lead the pitch with what participants will learn and how they will benefit

- Include a two to three-minute video sample of your program. The video should solely highlight your speaking content

- Consider pitching (or re-pitching) your programming around a themed month or season

- Get the prospective client on the phone to inquire about their needs and be open to tailoring your program to their needs

9 Ways to Research Campus Needs:

1. Ask college staff/ faculty about current issues on their campus.

2. Interview student leaders about their learning gap.

3. Follow campus leadership programs and take note of the sponsored programming.

4. Ask a fellow speaker in the college market about college trends.

5. Set up Google alerts with college trends as the keyword and stay in the know about campus culture.

6. Attend higher education-related conferences to learn the lingo and evolution of post-secondary culture.

7. Increase your network of college professors and ask them to forward proposal solicitations.

8. Join your local colleges' list serve to stay in the know about upcoming events.

Speak Up!

9. Attend local college events related to your area of expertise.

You have got the juice! Start your research, tailor your targeted messaging, and start soliciting proposals! Included below is a list of conferences to help you get started:

Conferences to Consider

1. National Conference for College Women Student Leaders (NCCWSL)

2. National Association for Campus Activities (NACA)

3. Coalition for Collegiate Women's Leadership (CCWL)

4. Association of Fraternal Leadership & Values (AFLV) Central

5. Association of Fraternal Leadership & Values (AFLV) west

6. OWN IT Summit

7. Northeast Greek Leadership Association

8. National Student Leadership Diversity Convention

9. Advanced Leadership Development in Higher Education

10. American Council on Education

11. NAFSA Annual Conference & Expo

12. Advanced Leadership Development in Higher Education

13. Institute on High-Impact Practices and Student Success

14. International Conference of Education – San Francisco

15. Association of Texas College & University Facilities Professionals

16. Advancing Improvement in Education

17. National Conference on Student Leadership

LINNITA HOSTEN

Award-winning keynote speaker and college success strategist, Linnita Hosten, is the author of The College Strategy - a toolkit to support students in creating a college success plan to maximize the college experience.

Linnita's work with students began at age 19 as a recreation summer camp counselor and expanded through numerous roles to include: Resident assistant, orientation team leader, cheerleading coach, private tutor, college advisor, personal mentor, and college professor.

The high-energy edutainer provides content-packed and research-based success strategy programming for organizations, universities, and community groups.

Linnita's passion for success strategy also extends beyond traditional students to supporting military personnel, Job Corp participants and returning citizens.

Her achievements have been recognized by the Prince George's County Social Innovation Fund, University of Maryland University College Alumni Association, Indie Author Legacy Awards, and more.

Linnita received a Bachelor of Science degree in Mass Communication from Towson University and a Master of

Science degree in Nonprofit Management and Association Leadership from the University of Maryland University College.

When not on stage, you can find the pescatarian in the produce section at Wegmans; browsing online for the perfect fit; diving in a good book or enjoying the company of her favorite college mentee - her sister, Makenzie.

Linnita's mission is to ensure that every student leaves their campus with confidence and the skill set to define and reach their definition of success.

www.linnitahosten.com
www.twitter.com/linnitahosten
www.facebook.com/linnitahostenofficial
www.instagram.com/linnitahosten

SPEAKING IS MORE THAN SPEAKING!
DEVELOPING THE MINDSET OF A PROFESSIONAL SPEAKER

DR. WILL MORELAND

Speaking Is Serious Business

Your message is someone's medicine! Let that sink in. Read it one more time. Your message is someone's medicine!

Think about the biggest movements in the world. The Civil Rights Movement was sparked by words. Dr. Martin Luther King Jr. used words to bring awareness and support to the cause of civil rights for all people. Christianity and all other religious movements have been spread by using words.

As a Professional Speaker, I believe that you have the power to Impact, Inspire and Influence thousands of people with your message. Think about a time when you were down and out, needed a pick me up. You most likely turned to someone's message of hope and inspiration. The same thing is true when you want to be pumped up, you listened to someone's motivating words. That is why I believe your words can be someone's medicine.

When a person is feeling dehydrated, they will be given an intravenous injection, we call it an I.V. for short. An I.V. is used because it is the fastest way to deliver the needed fluid to the body. As a Speaker, your words can be the needed fluid that reaches a person's heart, soul, and mind. Giving them the encouragement, they need.

I often tell my coaching clients that as a Professional Speaker, I regard what we do in the same way I would think of a Heart Surgeon. I know you may think that is a drastic statement, but consider for a moment, just as important it would be to give someone a new heart, our fix their heart, the same is true, when we change someone's perspective on life. Give them hope to keep living. Many people have contacted me to share that they were ready to end their life, but something I said, changed their mind.

As Professional Speakers, we give "Life Transplants."

Maybe you are not sharing what you would consider life-changing information, maybe you are using speaking to share a product or service you provide. I believe you can still bring that same passion if you truly believe in the product or service you are offering.

THINK LIKE A PRO

Being a Professional Speaker is one of the most rewarding professions on the planet and one of the highest paying when done right. A beginning Speaker can easily request $2,000 - $3,000 per talk. Speaking anywhere from 20 to 30 times a year can prove to be very profitable. Top Speakers can request anywhere from \$7,500 - \$15,000 per speaking opportunity.

Although building a Speaker Business can be profitable, most Speakers struggle and never get their business off the ground. They will experience an opportunity here and there, but nothing on a consistent basis.

Why is that? I mean, it is rewarding and pays well. Why do most Speakers fail?

Simply put, they run their Speaker Business as a hobby and not as a business. If you are going to have success as a Professional Speaker, you need to become a PRO. I created this acronym for my clients to help them stay on track to building their speaker business.

Let's break down this acronym and get you on the path to building a rewarding and successful Speaking Business.

THE "P" IN PRO

As a Speaker, you want to be Precise in key areas of your business. Precise is another word for clear. Who is your target audience? Who can benefit the most from your message? Think back to my reference, your message is someone's medicine. But everyone cannot take the same medicine. There is medicine for children, adults, and elders. Who is your message for? If you were a sex therapist, you wouldn't market your service to elementary schools. Some medicines you cannot buy over the counter, maybe your message is a unique targeted message. You need to be precise about that.

THE "R" IN PRO

Here is where most Speakers will lose the game. Building a Speaker Business is all about repetitious practices done over and over daily. As an example, you may need to send out 25 emails a day to get in front of your ideal target market. At the same time, you need to have a strong marketing strategy to continuously tell your story to the market place. To have a successful business, you need to have systems in place that allow you to stay current on all your daily tasks. I tell my clients all of the time, success is boring. The rewards are exciting, but the process is boring.

THE "O" IN PRO

Just like any business, you will have your ups and downs. You must stay focused on the overall goal. The result of you helping thousands of people with your message, service, or product. Having a positive attitude is a must for any Entrepreneur. If you are not optimistic about your success, it will not happen for you and you will not enjoy the journey. I know the work I put in daily, so when I get my desired results, it feels that much better.

BUILD A BUSINESS YOU LOVE

The PRO Formula is a great starting place to build your Professional Speaking Business. Having those three basics in place will serve you well.

Speak Up!

Being an Entrepreneur gives you an opportunity to design a life and business you love. You literally get to build it in a way that supports your lifestyle. Speaking has allowed me to build an amazing life. Because of that, I honor the profession and give my best efforts.

As you continue to read and re-read this awesome tool to help you build your Speaking Business. Move forward with confidence knowing that you have what it takes to Impact, Inspire, and Influence thousands and even millions of people.

Your voice could be the spark that some young woman needs to hear to inspire her to become more than she ever dreamed possible. Your voice could be the voice that moves some young man to become a better man for his family. Your voice could be the voice that influences a Nation to become better.

I truly believe that "Your Message Is Someone's Medicine." Take what you do seriously and become a PRO to reach your target audience.

DR. WILL MORELAND
America's #1 Leadership Life Trainer

Few speakers have had the global success Dr. Will has achieved as a Speaker. Speaking in over 40 Countries, Impacting, Inspiring, and Influencing audiences around the world with his keynotes and books. Dr. Will is a bestselling author and has written over 40 books. He is the founder of Genius Speakers Academy where he trains other Speakers to build thriving speaking businesses and amplify their voice.

Dr. Will is committed to raising the impact Speakers have around the world, because he truly believes that the Speaking Industry is vital to the success of communities, countries, and continents.

A favorite quote of Dr. Will's...
"Inspired people lead inspired lives!"

Dr. Will was named a Top Speaker in America and continues to make a global impact daily.

www.drwillspeaks.com
www.twitter.com/drwillspeaks
www.instagram.com/drwillspeaks
www.snapchat.com/drwillspeaks

Message!

In this section you will learn what type of speaker you are and refine your core presentation skills

SO, YOU THINK YOU ARE READY FOR A TEDX TALK?

HORACE BUDDOO

"So, you think you are ready for a TEDx Talk[1]"? That is the question I often ask clients who come to me for TEDx speaker coaching. The response is usually a "Yeah! Duh! That is why I am here!" along with a facial expression that makes me think they are starting to question my intelligence and their decision to seek my help. It is not that I am doubting their ability to speak well and deliver something amazing. Most of the clients who come to me are people who are experienced in the world of public speaking. However, it has been my consistent experience as a TEDx speaker coach that many people really have no clue what being "ready for a TEDx Talk" actually entails. Being ready for the TEDx stage starts way before you even apply to give a talk. It starts way before you take pen to paper (or fingertips to keyboard) to write your talk. It starts with both your intention and your idea itself.

It is no secret that being on a TEDx stage can do wonders for your career. Mel Robbins' TEDx talk, "How to Stop Screwing Yourself Over" has accumulated more than 17

---

[1] Please go to my website at www.useyourspeak.com/speakupbook for extra resources and more information about how to deliver unforgettable TEDx Talks.

million views on YouTube and helped to launch her best seller entitled "The 5-Second Rule". Clint Smith's TEDx Talk "Celebrating Resilience: Reframing the Narrative Around Our Students" helped to bring awareness to his message which helped him to get on the main TED stage at least twice garnering more than a million views on YouTube. With that level of viewership potential, there is no doubt that all of that could be leveraged to help gain credibility in a particular area of expertise, exposure to your target audience, and bookings based on the two aforementioned. But if your TEDx Talk aspirations are grounded in potential financial gain, I would emphatically say that you would be the wrong candidate to give a TEDx Talk, and as a TEDx organizer, I would pass right over your application if I got any sense that your goals are self-serving. Even though for some speakers, credibility, exposure, and bookings increased as a result of giving a TEDx Talk, these should not be your primary reasons for speaking on a TEDx stage. So again, I will ask the question, "So you think you are ready for a TEDx Talk?"

During my coaching sessions with potential TEDx speakers, I often have them go through an exercise which gets them to take a true introspective look at their motives and intentions so that they can evaluate their "why." Why do you want to give a TEDx Talk? The TED tagline is "ideas worth spreading" and the TED Organization has very loose but intentional standards of what those types of ideas should look like. But whatever that idea is, you always want it to be something that will draw attention and "make some noise." I have created the acronym **D.R.U.M** to help you measure if your idea is indeed one that is worth spreading on a TEDx stage.

First, your idea should be **DEFENDABLE**. It should be something that research, science, or anecdotal stories can support.

Secondly, it should be **RELATABLE**. Your idea should be something that will resonate with the masses, even though it may not be applicable to everyone.

Thirdly, your idea should be **UNIQUE** to the TED/TEDx stage. What I mean by unique is that your idea should never be a regurgitation of another previously delivered TEDx Talk. Therefore, it is important for you to do research to see if your idea has ever been delivered on a TEDx platform before.

Lastly, and most importantly, your idea should be **MIND-CHANGING**. It should change the thoughts and perceptions of those who encounter it either by inspiring them to act or at the very least, by sparking meaningful conversations.

The idea should be impactful enough for them to see something in a new way. It is with these standards in mind that you should measure your ideas because a TEDx Talk is always about the idea, not the speaker. So again, I will ask the question, "So you think you are ready for a TEDx Talk?"

My TEDx organizing, coaching, curating, and general fandom for TEDx talks have taught me so much about the nuanced differences between TEDx speaking and other types of public speaking. I find that many potential TEDx speakers who are used to doing other types of public speaking may not necessarily be aware of these important nuances that make a TEDx Talk different. Sometimes potential speakers have to be coached out of their keynote speaking habits in order to be a good fit for TEDx. We have to remember that even though developing the right idea is important, knowing how to effectively deliver that idea on a TEDx stage is just as important. So, let's compare and contrast how a TEDx Talk is different from regular talks.

- **Time**: TEDx Talks are a maximum of 18 minutes long as compared to a keynote which usually lasts an average of 45 minutes to an hour.

- **Style:** TEDx Talks are a bit more conversational and involves more understated and natural types of gestures that do not necessarily incite audience feedback. Other types of talks may involve a more bombastic delivery with more exaggerated gestures and may involve more of a "back and forth" between the speaker and the audience of which TEDx Talks do not usually have.

- **Content:** TEDx Talks are focused on one pervasive idea that is developed throughout the talk whereas other types of talks, such as keynotes, may touch on multiple points and ideas.

- **Purpose:** TEDx Talks are about delivering a well-informed talk for the purpose of spreading an amazing idea whereas other types of talks may serve multiple purposes which include self-promotion and monetary gain.

- **Ownership:** When you do a TEDx Talk, you are gifting your talk to the masses - literally. You cannot be paid to give a TEDx Talk. You also do not own your TEDx Talk and cannot monetize it. TEDx Talks are all licensed under Creative Commons which gives the TED Organization the right to use your talk in any way they deem fit. Whereas your individual talks elsewhere can potentially be individually monetized, copyrighted, and used in ways that are not as limiting. TEDx Talks are not set up that way.

So, what makes a good TEDx Talk? There has been a lot written about his topic but even Chris Anderson himself, who is the head of the TED Organization, would tell you that there is no one formula that dictates what a good TEDx Talk should look like. I like to tell my clients to not think in terms of recipes but in terms of ingredients. There are three basic ingredients that I believe every TEDx Talk should have and how this oratorical "meal" is prepared will depend on the individual.

- **Compelling Idea:** Your talk should make the audience want to do something, experience something, discuss something, or change something.

- **Good Storytelling:** Your talk should use imagery and multisensory experiences to connect both intellectually and emotionally with the audience.

- **Authentic Delivery:** You should always be true to the integrity of your talk fearlessly convey your most

authentic self. Sometimes showing vulnerability will
be necessary for the connectivity

Your audience is not only the people in front of you but those
who will be watching the talk online after the talk is posted to
the TEDx YouTube channel. In fact, I would venture to say
that the online watchers are your primary audience so your
idea, storytelling, and delivery have to be engaging enough to
capture the attention of the person who can easily click to
another video if disinterested as opposed to merely the
person who may have paid money to attend the live event
and will probably sit and listen no matter how engaging you
may or may not be.

There are many other facets of TEDx speaking that simply
cannot be addressed in one chapter alone, so I chose to
address what I thought was the most important. But you may
have many other questions such as:

- What are the various types of TEDx Talks that I can
  potentially do?

- What is the difference between TED and TEDx?

- How do I use the standard of D.R.U.M (Defendable,
  Relatable, Unique, Mind-changing) to come up with
  my compelling idea?

- How do I successfully apply to do a TEDx Talk?

- How do I increase my chances of landing a TEDx
  Talk?

- What are the Do's and Don'ts of delivering a TEDx
  Talk?

- What do I do after I have delivered my TEDx Talk?

I am sure you have even more questions that were not mentioned above. I highly recommend that you visit www.useyourspeak.com/speakupbook so that you can get all your questions answered and find valuable resources to help make your TEDx Talk dream a reality.

Let me now ask myself the question of the hour: "Do I think that YOU are ready for a TEDx Talk? Absolutely! I definitely think you are ready for the TEDx journey!"

HORACE BUDDOO

Horace is a communication coach, speaker, TEDx organizer, and author who specializes in teaching clients the skills of successful public speaking and the skills necessary to have open and honest conversations. These are important and effective tools for those who seek to advance their careers and effectively communicate ideas in a way that will enhance professional and personal relationships.

He has coached CEOs, TV personalities, and numerous professionals who seek to improve the communication skills necessary for life success. He has also led master classes on public speaking and effective conversations and is currently working on a book entitled "The Mindful Speaker" that will teach both novice and master speakers how to mindfully elevate their communication skills to achieve success in any area of their lives.

Horace has been the organizer and curator of two successful TEDx events and consulted on other TEDx events as well. He has coached scores of TEDx speakers and helped them to craft and deliver extraordinary TEDx Talks.

Horace's coaching approach is grounded in Sociology and Anthropology, of which he has two degrees respectively. His methods are based on well-researched ideas, but he finds a way to make it very practical so that the lessons can be easily adapted and applied to any type of interaction and to any level of communication. Because Horace believes that the ability to communicate will determine the quality of personal or professional relationships, he is passionate about equipping people with the communication skills necessary to improve their lives.

www.useyourspeak.com
www.instagram.com/useyourspeak
www.instagram.com/horacebuddoo
www.twitter.com/horacebuddoo

IT IS NOT ALL ABOUT THE KEYNOTE!

HOW TO LEVERAGE BEING AN EMCEE, MODERATOR OR PANELIST SPEAKER

KIAUNDRA JACKSON

Standing on a stage with hundreds or even thousands of attendees giving you their undivided attention for a sustained amount of time is a feeling like none other. While being a keynote speaker has some exceptional perks and can develop a "speaker muscle" you did not even know you had, there are other roles you can participate in as a speaker that will help you develop your skillset even further. Being an emcee, moderator, or a panelist is a much different experience than being a keynote speaker but can provide an equal or even greater opportunity if done correctly. Let's dive deeper into what being an emcee, moderator, and panelist speaker entails.

An emcee (also known as a MC, Master of Ceremony) is defined as a facilitator of an event. It can be a wedding, a party, seminar, workshop, or a conference. As an emcee, you have the capacity to control a room and prepare them for the program ahead. Your energy, level of excitement, interaction with the crowd, and ability to keep them engaged rests in your hands. You set the tone for introducing everyone on the program and how you choose to do it really matters.

Have you ever been at an event and the emcee is so boring that you lose attention? Or the attendees start to have side conversations because they are no longer engaged?

Well, that is exactly what you do not want to ever happen to you. There is an art to it. You not only have to adlib, but you have to be a little more spontaneous too. It is imperative to pay close attention to what the other speakers and acts do during their presentation, so you can weave that into the short time you have in between the speakers.

Here are 7 quick tips to help you leverage being an emcee:

1. **Have an engaging opening.** You set the tone for the entire event, so make it exciting.

2. **Remember, it is not all about you.** Attendees came to hear and see the other individuals on the program.

3. **Control the time.** Being too quick or too slow can throw off the entire schedule.

4. **Dress accordingly.** Depending on the event, make sure you are dressed like the attendees. If it is a very formal event, a suit, tie, or gown may be a great option.

5. **Have good transitions between the different parts of the program to avoid dead air.** Pay attention to the other acts to make sure your transitions are relevant.

6. **Be prepared if you or anyone should make a mistake.** Mistakes will happen, but you have to learn how to recover quickly.

7. **Prepare a good closing for the event.** Keep the same level of excitement all the way to the end.

A moderator is the person who is in charge of a particular discussion and makes sure it is conducted in a fair and organized manner. We often hear the term, moderator, when dealing with panel discussions. It is your responsibility to keep the panelists on track with the subject matter and time. When the moderator of a panel is amazing, it makes for a great panel discussion because everything flows well even when members of the panel are not as on target as they should be. There is always room for the moderator to quickly seed their products, services, and expertise as a bridge to intertwine the panelist's comments or responses. It is imperative for the moderator to know the ins and outs of their topic and to know everything you can about the panelists and their background.

One of the best panels I ever moderated was at the Los Angeles Convention Center. I had some heavy hitters on my panel which included the COO of the Los Angeles Spark, Talent Acquisition from 20th Century Fox, and a Bank Executive who fundraised over 3 million dollars. I did massive research on all of them leading up to the panel discussion to make sure I knew who I should direct certain questions to and who can give the most value to the audience.

Here are some quick tips I used to help leverage being a moderator:

1. I did not allow the panelist to introduce themselves in the interest of time

2. I over-prepared on purpose

3. I did not let a panelist go off topic

4. I stayed on time

5. I briefly seeded being a therapist and owning a private practice for mental health services

6. I prepared 20+ questions to ask the panelists based on our topic

7. I took a few questions from the audience at the end

Being a panelist speaker provides the opportunity for you and other individuals to be in front of an audience discussing and answering questions on a particular topic, which is led by a panel moderator. Being a panelist is a great way to quickly showcase your expertise on a particular topic. The key elements of being a great panelist are: not to be boring and not to hog up all the time. I cannot tell you how many panel discussions have bored me due to the lack of engagement, panelist talking for too long, getting off topic, and the moderator not being able to navigate time appropriately. Please do not let that be you. As a panelist you should answer or comment briefly. Make sure you are concise, quick, and to the point.

I would highly recommend speaking in sound bites. Sound bites are often used in the media but are short phrases or sentences that capture the essence of what the speaker is trying to say. It is used to summarize information and entice the listener to want more. If you ever see a line of people waiting to talk to a particular person after the panel discussion has ended--they provided valuable information, but left the listeners wanting more.

Here are some quick tips I used to help leverage being a panelist:

1. **Disagree once.** No one wants to listen to a panel where there is no difference of opinion.

2. **Use soundbites.** Quick short sentences that clarify your point but leaves the audience wanting more.

3. **Use acronyms.** Use a short 3-4 letter word to further explain your point (Ex: S.T.A.G.E).

4. **Be prepared.** Make sure you are knowledgeable on the topic.

5. **Do not talk for too long.** The other panelists want to speak as well. Be respectful of their time.

6. **Do not be boring.** Use hand movements, changes in tone of voice and quick stories to reiterate your talking points.

7. **Be available for questions after.** Carve out time to stay a few minutes after to answer any questions attendees may have.

The next time you are asked to be an emcee, moderator, or panelist speaker, I hope you will jump at the amazing opportunity to use the art of speaking in a new and exciting way. Doing a keynote is known as one of the best ways to get paid as a speaker. Keep in mind the options we just discussed can be just as lucrative in obtaining new clients, adding individuals to your email list, selling books, and booking other speaking engagements. Just remember, it is not all about the keynote!

If you are ready to uncover your true potential and learn more about how to maximize being a speaker, visit:

www.KiaundraJackson.com

KIAUNDRA JACKSON

 Kiaundra Jackson is known as America's #1 Relationship Therapist. She has been seen on the Emmy-Award Winning TV Show, The Doctors. She has been recently featured in The New York Times, BET, FOX, The CW, Vice and The Huffington Post as one of the '10 Black Female Therapists You Should Know.' She is an international speaker, 4x author, and a trusted Licensed Marriage and Family Therapist that gets results. She is a noted expert on mental health, healthy relationships and is passionate about equipping new and emerging speakers.

Kiaundra currently owns a thriving private practice in Los Angeles. Among her areas of expertise are: Premarital and Marital issues, Anxiety, Depression, Life Transition, Grief, Loss, and Faith Based Counseling. Her therapeutic approach is holistic, eclectic, and tailored to her clients' needs, making sure each person is cared for biologically, emotionally, and spiritually.

Through her early work, she discovered the importance of having healthy relationships. From that point on, she chose to specialize in helping couples strengthen and repair their relationships.

Kiaundra's vision is to help 100,000 couples heal their relationships, prevent divorce, and keep families together.

www.facebook.com/KWCouplesTherapy
www.instagram.com/KiaundraJackson
www.twitter.com/KiaundraJackson

SLAY THE STAGE!

WHY A POWERFUL KEYNOTE IS YOUR #1 ASSET

ROQUITA JOHNSON

You have been asked to give a keynote speech.
Congratulations! It really is an honor to be the keynote
speaker for an event. You have the awesome opportunity to
drive home the theme of the event, fire attendees up, and
provide a message that will impact lives long after you have
left the stage. In other words – it is kind of a big deal! A
keynote that is delivered masterfully is a win for both the
person(s)/organization hosting the event and the speaker.
Before we talk about why every serious speaker needs to
have a powerful keynote as part of their speaking arsenal,
let's first define what this type of speech is and is *not.*

A keynote presentation is typically given at the beginning of
a conference or meeting and sets the tone for the event. Think
about the meaning of keynote in music lingo – It is the
leading note in a musical key. It sets the tone for how the rest
of the song will be performed. This is the same idea behind a
keynote speech; its main message embodies the event's
theme and lets attendees know what they can expect to learn
during their time there. It is informative, entertaining, and
motivational. Audience members should feel inspired to
think differently, consider a new perspective, or do
something in a better way. What a keynote is *not* is a

workshop, breakout session, or speaker panel. It presents *and* represents the grand, overarching vision for the attendees. So, you can see why the keynote is integral to the success of an event!

As you can probably tell, keynote speakers are not chosen lightly. If your name is brought up during the planning committee's discussion, rest assured it is because they believe you possess the expertise and experience necessary to fulfill their vision. Organizers also want someone who can boost the public profile of their event, so that is why you will often see celebrities as the headlining act. They might have no (apparent) connection to the conference theme but may be chosen because their name will attract a large crowd. This is a big perk of being the keynote speaker – while you are helping the organizers to draw attendees, you are also gaining a massive amount of publicity in your own right. But what exactly goes into a powerful keynote?

For starters, you need to have a message that you care about. Believe me, when you are genuinely excited about your message, the audience can feel it from the stage. What lights you on fire? What is something you talk about passionately? What message would you talk about even if no one paid you for it? There is a message within you that addresses a need someone has; the kind of message that will positively impact someone's life and be the catalyst for their paradigm shift.

When creating your keynote (or any presentation), always keep this in mind: only have ONE core message. On more than one occasion, I have listened to a speech and left confused at the end because I could not determine what the speaker's main message was. Was it about focusing on my goals during times of stress? The importance of creating a goal-oriented dream team? Cultivating my dream life? It should be very clear to the audience what the point of your talk is. If someone asked an attendee what your speech was about, they should be able to sum it up in a succinct sentence.

To separate yourself from the pack when creating your keynote message, I recommend having a unique angle on a topic. When you think of how many people speak on the same topics, you start to understand why it is important to carve out your own lane. Perhaps you speak on relationships, but you express an interesting (or controversial) viewpoint not heard before. Do not be afraid to be different!

Next, your powerful keynote needs to include a story. Who does not love a story? They have been told since the beginning of time and transcend cultures and countries. Most people can relate to a story that has a universal theme. You might be thinking "I do not have any stories interesting enough for a speech." That is absolutely not true! Our lives are composed of defining moments and observations that have changed us in some way, and that is where you will often find those messages that matter the most. If you have ever noticed, the most in-demand keynote speakers all have a signature story that they include in almost every keynote speech. Les Brown's "Mamie Brown's Baby Boy/Radio DJ" story is legendary. I bet if you took a poll on who tells the "No Baby Diapers/Funding My Dream" story, people in the know would tell you it is Lisa Nichols. They are best known for these stories. Why do Les' and Lisa's stories resonate with people so much? Because they are motivational stories of overcoming real-life challenges. People leave feeling empowered to change the direction of their life. If Les and Lisa can create a new reality, they can too. Stories have the power to build a personal connection with audience members, touch their emotions in a way that facts and statistics cannot, and play an essential part in supporting your main message. Always include stories in your keynote.

Visual aids are another powerful tool to consider. They should, however, only be used if they benefit your presentation in some way. Will they make the abstract clearer? Demonstrate how a procedure is done? Help explain a process better? Personally, I am a big fan of props! If you can show me better than you can tell me, I am all for it. Again, the visual aid needs to serve a purpose. One of my favorite props used in a presentation were the mosquitoes Bill Gates unleashed during his famous TED talk titled "Mosquitoes, Malaria, and Education." Do not worry, the mosquitoes were harmless. They were also extremely effective because audience members were instantly put in the shoes of someone who lives among malaria-infected mosquitoes every day. Bill definitely brought the element of surprise with this prop! It was closely related to his message, and you can easily see it was a hit (if not a shocking one) with the audience. I gave a speech about resilience where I used a rubber band as my prop. It was a simple prop, but also very effective as I stretched it to show how humans are stretched when dealing with crises – and how we revert back to our normal selves once the challenge has been dealt with.

Props do not have to be complicated or in the form of a PowerPoint deck. Be creative! Videos and sounds are other good options that will help you and your keynote stand out in people's minds.

So far, we have discussed having a clear message you care about, telling memorable stories, and using meaningful props. A powerful keynote also needs action. As in, a call to action that the audience can leave with. What do you want them to do, think, or feel? If your keynote is about living your best life, perhaps your charge to the audience is to write down three realistic ways they can get more productivity out of their days. If you're speaking on juvenile delinquency, you may ask each audience member to start actively building a positive relationship with a local at-risk youth by mentoring them. A good keynote speaker gives the listeners tactics throughout their speech to incorporate the message into their lives, and a specific call to action towards the end helps to anchor your message even more.

Ultimately, *you* make your keynote powerful. You are the differentiation factor. Your unique message, your honest point of view, the stories, and examples you use – all of this contributes to a speech that is authentically you. And this is exactly what the audience is looking for.

A powerful message can get your foot in the door as a keynote prospect and successfully delivering that message builds your reputation and rockets your credibility. This, of course, makes you that much more appealing to future clients who will want to hire you. When you know your stuff and can deliver in an engaging way – watch how people will start to seek YOU out!

ROQUITA JOHNSON

Roquita Johnson is an award-winning speaker, Certified World Class Speaking Coach, and founder and president of Roquita Johnson Public Speaking LLC. She has worked with a variety of people to develop and hone their speaking skills, specializing in serving faith-based speakers and business professionals. Her goal is not to change who a person authentically is, but instead – to bring out the BEST version of who they already are as a speaker. Through one-on-one and group coaching programs and workshops, she works with clients on storytelling, audience engagement, managing nerves and more. She is based out of Bridgeport, Connecticut and considers it a calling to help people "Slay the Stage!"

www.roquitajohnson.com
www.facebook.com/RoquitaJohnsonPublicSpeaking
www.instagram.com/roquitajohnson_publicspeaking

EDUCATE, ENTERTAIN, AND INSPIRE!

HOW TO TELL STORIES LIKE AWARD WINNING ACTORS

CLIFF TOWNSEND

"I have learned that people will forget what you said, people will forget what you did, but people will never forget how you made them feel"
Maya Angelou

This quote sums up the effect a memorable story has on its listener. People may forget your name or what you talked about, but the way your story made them feel goes with them forever.

Have you ever watched a movie and years later you forgot the name of the movie, what the movie was about, who starred in the movie, but there was this one scene that totally changed your perspective on something in your life, and you have never forgotten it, because of the way it made you feel?

Just like making a cake or your favorite dish, there are certain ingredients that movie makers use in order to impress upon your mind moments that are unforgettable, and the same goes for storytelling.

Hollywood and the entertainment industry have perfected the mastery of storytelling with all the right ingredients, and that is why consumers spend billions of dollars every year to watch and listen to them tell stories.

Here are the main ingredients that you will need in order to create an unforgettable story like Hollywood Actors and Directors.

Relatability: If they cannot imagine themselves in the situation then they probably cannot relate to the story.

Believable: Your listener must believe that not only is it possible, but it is possible for them.

Evocative: Your story must evoke strong feelings and emotions in your audience.

Purposeful: Your story must serve some kind of purpose or else there is no point in sharing it.

Inclusive: Your listener should be nodding in agreement or expressing approval by facial expressions because they are thinking to themselves, yes, me too.

Inspiring: All exceptional stories have the ability to inspire their audience to take a stand either for or against something.

THE 3 SECRET TECHNIQUES ALL MASTER STORYTELLERS USE

Secret #1... Distraction

Just like you and me, your listener has a million and one things going on in their mind at any given time. Studies show that the average person will have approximately 70,000 thoughts per day and the majority of those thoughts are negative.

Regardless of whether their thoughts are negative or positive you can see that they are preoccupied with things that are going on in their life. Just because they are in front of you does not mean that those distractions have automatically gone away. In order for you to be able to deliver a message that resonates and connects with them on an emotional level you need to distract them from their own thoughts.

Your job as a Speaker-Coach-Trainer is to take temporary control of their mind. Your job is to take away whatever is currently distracting them so they are present in the moment.

There are different distraction techniques and whichever one you decide to use is dependent upon the situation. For example, asking a question forces your listener to start thinking about the subject you asked about, others may state a shocking statistic, or make an outrageous or shocking statement.

The best time to distract your audience and grab their attention is in your opening, just like in the movies they usually start with an opening that grabs your attention and keeps you on the edge of your seat to the end.

A surprise attack, a crash, an outrageous act that would go against most people's moral fiber, anything that engages your audience immediately and takes them away from their normal everyday routine can be a distraction technique.

Secret #2… Dispute

Your audience has pre-determined beliefs about most things, including whatever topic you will be sharing with them. Those beliefs are based on the experiences they have had, their upbringing, their neighborhood, their peers, schools, parents, church, culture, gender, race, and everything else you can possibly think of.

It is your job to dispute those lifelong beliefs and implant innovative ideas and beliefs in their mind. It is usually not a good idea to dispute other people's beliefs without offering very strong supportive evidence, because most people will literally fight you to keep their beliefs even when they know that it is not in their best interest and does not support their growth.

They will fight to keep those ideas. Even though they know the ideas do not serve them well, they are the only ones they have, and they will fight to protect them because they have held them for most of their life, and they feel they would be lost without them.

The best way to dispute someone's belief and have them accept or be open to a new way of thinking is to first use yourself as the example and build supportive evidence with your real-life example. However, it must be something that they can relate to.

Whatever belief you want to implant in your listener's mind, you must first give a personal example of when you were in their shoes. Give an example of when you had the same belief and how it kept you from achieving certain things. However, your breakthrough came from discovering this new way of thinking and since you have adopted this new way of thinking, your life has changed for the better. Theirs will change also once they start to abandon their old way of thinking and adopt this new and improved belief.

By adopting this technique of using yourself as the example and asking a few agreeable questions, they automatically give you permission to dispute their old belief and to share your new belief.

Secret #3... Inspire

Now that you have distracted your audience with an amazing opening to your story and you have disputed their old belief system, What is next?

The next thing you must do is inspire your listener to do something with the latest information or belief that you have imprinted in their mind.

You have given them a new tool that they are eager and ready to put it to use. Now it is your job to inspire them to take some type of action.

This is usually where you inspire them to act on whatever your call to action is. Do you want them to take the next step in your coaching program and build on this new belief? Do you want them to sign a petition or go out and vote? What do you want to inspire them to do? Now is the time to do it.

3 KEYS TO EFFECTIVE STORYTELLING

Key #1... Be Authentic

You have distracted, disputed, and inspired your audience; however, those techniques will not work unless you are being authentic. Being authentic is the biggest characteristic you can have as a master storyteller.

If you are not authentic your listener will sense it and they will shut you out. When that happens, you have lost them for good, not just at that moment but forever. Being authentic means being yourself and not pretending to be someone that you are not.

Key #2... Emotional Vulnerability

This is the secret sauce to mastering storytelling. This is also the most difficult for most people. The more emotionally vulnerable you are the more you can connect with your audience, however this comes with a word of caution.

There is a fine line when it comes to being emotionally vulnerable. DO NOT USE YOUR AUDIENCE AS YOUR THERAPIST. This rule should NEVER be broken.

You should never tell a story that will allow you to lose control of your emotions. You should go to the edge of the cliff but do not jump off.

Any story that will bring you to that point should be practiced and practiced and practiced until you can tell the story with a level of control. I say a level of control because you want your emotions to be real because your audience will sense if it is not, however the audience is not there to console you as the storyteller if you break down, they are there to learn from you.

Key #3… Creating An Alter Ego

There are times when a certain character is needed to deliver a story, but you may not be that type of person. However, as they say in Hollywood, the show must go on and your story must also go on. How do you fulfill your obligation to your audience when you are not that person?

Creating an alter ego is the way to do it. Every time you are telling a story you are performing, and you should be in performance mode. What character do you need to be to deliver your story, if it is not who you are naturally then create that character.

Creating an alter ego allows you to become the person you need to be in order to fulfill your obligation to your audience. This is the same way that Hollywood's best actors create alter egos in order to fulfill their obligation to us as movie audiences.

Cliff Townsend

 Cliff Townsend is an award-winning Actor-Director and Writer. As an Actor-Writer and filmmaker Cliff has studied and worked with some of the best in the industry.

He has learned firsthand the secrets, techniques, and strategies that award-winning actors use to tell stories.

Cliff has also worked and trained with some of the best speakers - entertainers and Storytellers in the business including legendary speaker Les Brown and was one of the founding partners of the Les Brown Institute.

Today Cliff shares those secrets, techniques, and strategies with private coaching clients and also with people across the globe who have a story to tell through his online platform SpeakingMasteryAcademy.com

www.linkedin.com/in/clifftownsend
www.instagram.com/speaking_mastery_academy
www.facebook.com/speakercoaching

Marketing!

*In this section, you will develop strategies to reach
and engage your target audience*

ATTRACT NATIONAL TELEVISION NETWORK ATTENTION!

THE INS AND OUTS OF A NATIONAL PRESS RELEASE AND PITCH

CRYSTAL I. BERGER

"Keep it simple stupid..." is a phrase that my favorite instructor used every day while I was attending broadcasting school. Many of my classmates (myself included) thought our professor was being distasteful in his language. It was not until my first day on the job at a national television network that I learned the value of concise, direct, and simple language.

Producers, bookers, assignment editors, and media executives are some of the busiest people on the planet. They work tirelessly to deliver quality content to millions of consumers within seconds. Most do not have the time or energy to make sense of your media pitch. For that reason alone, you only get a few seconds - about 30 of them to be exact - to ensure that your message matters to their viewer and listener base. Get right down to the good stuff when pitching and quickly highlight how your message and brand can make their shows and programming, not just better, but the best!

Before drafting your national attention-grabbing press release, here are five (5) essential questions to ponder:

1. Am I pitching to the *right* platform for my message and brand?

2. Is my press pitch/release newsworthy *and* timely?

3. Are my talking points so immediately clear that anyone can see the benefit(s) of having me on their show?

4. Have I included up-to-date, easy to find, contact information in my press release?

5. Did I *keep it simple* enough that even the *'stupidest'* person can immediately see who I am and why what I have to say matters?

Now that you have answered those essential questions, let's begin drafting your national network attention-grabbing press release. But first, let me rewind. You may be asking yourself, "why does she keep saying *national attention-grabbing* press release?" Well, one of the biggest mistakes that novice experts make is pitching their brand and message with a local angle. This is a fool-proof way to prevent you from being considered for national shows. If your pitch seems too regional or does not speak to your knowledge base as an expert that can speak to a national audience, network bookers will not consider your contribution until they feel you are ready for the big time.

Take a moment to assess if your message will speak to *all people*, not just people within your home state. Ask yourself, "is my message and expertise relevant from Georgia to Alaska and then over to Southern California?" If the answer is yes, you can put your fingers to the keypad and start drafting your press release. If the answer is *no*, then identify how you can mold your message to fit outside of a regional box. Be sure when shaping your message that you are not misleading or overreaching your skills, knowledge, and expertise. Producers and bookers are trained to see through embellishments and will quickly add your name to the "do not book" list... and yes, that list does exist! Be okay with not being ready. In that time, do more strategic press appearances outside of your local market to perfect your nation press pitch and message.

Back to drafting your *national network attention-grabbing press release* - I promise I will not say that tongue twister again in this chapter. The key to writing a successful press release is to grab the reader's attention with a headline that explains everything the reader needs to know within the first paragraph. Yes, within the first paragraph! Remember: press pitching is different than pitching your product release or event; the aforementioned types of pitches usually have local appeal.

To help journalists differentiate your press release from other communications they receive, adhere to the following seven elements that will structure any newsworthy release that you write.

An eye-catching headline. First, the press release must have an eye-catching headline. This should grab the reader's attention immediately and give a brief overview of why what you have to say is newsworthy - interesting, topical, notable, significant, and sometimes sensational. Here is a checklist of questions that will confirm if your pitch/press release is newsworthy:

1. *Is my message timely?* The word news means just that: things new and now. Are the topics you address current? Will the viewer and/or listener receive the latest updates and perspective from your message? Remember, most news goes bad quickly - almost as fast as a sliced avocado - so update your releases regularly so they do not get discarded for being stale.

2. *Is my perspective significant?* Again, does your perspective and message touch people outside of your local market? You want to be certain that the number of people you will influence is vast. *Note: the closer to home the perspective, the more newsworthy it is *locally*. Nationally, you want to ensure that your message touches the masses.

3. *Do you have a prominent perspective?* It is true that famous people get more coverage just because they are famous. You want to be sure that your message has been tested in lots of markets and your perspective holds authority that can, more often times than not, be Googled.

4. *Does your message grab the interest and the hearts of the people watching and listening?* Be sure to infuse how your story plays into your expertise. This will make your perspective more desired, unique, impactful and you guessed it, newsworthy.

Here's a quick example of a newsworthy headline:
'Baltimore Native Encourages People to BE the Change They Want to See' in their communities with the release of her book "Be Extraordinary: Claiming a Life of Purpose, Passion and Prosperity." This press pitch was sent out nationally as a response to addressing the systemic issues major cities face in light of the Freddie Gray case.

Second, ***readily available media contact information.*** The name, phone number, email, mailing address, and other contact information for the person who is distributing the release to the media must be visible and accurate. No one is going to search to find the contact person who should have been highlighted in your release.

Third, ***is the dateline***. This is in the first line of the first paragraph containing the release date, the city, and state. It is important for journalists to know they are receiving the most up-to-date information, even if you wrote the release a few days ago, put the date you are distributing the release.

Fourth, ***the introduction paragraph***. This is the most important paragraph because it may be the only part of the release that journalist bother to read. It must give the answers to who, what, where, why, and when. It is also important to have all key information given in the beginning and subsequent information should follow in order of diminishing importance. This is called the *Inverted Pyramid* style of writing.

Fifth, **the body**. This section can consist of two to several paragraphs. Here is where you explain details, statistics, background, talking points, and other relevant information. Highlight the uniqueness of your business - what differentiates you from your competitors. If you cannot think of a unique thing about your company - wait until you can before you send out the release. Be sure to continue following the inverted pyramid style. Remember, some readers will not ever make it to the end of your release, so order your points strategically.

Sixth, *the boilerplate*. This is a short paragraph about you and/or your company. In this paragraph, provide relevant background information that will set your message and brand apart from thousands of other pitchers. Be sure to include key media appearances, national brand affiliations, notable awards and recognition and years of experience in your industry.

Finally, *the close*. Have you ever wondered why the three pound symbols "###" are a standard practice for the close of a press release? Well, according to Wikipedia, the traditional symbol "-30-" was first used to signal "the end" or "over and out." This came from Civil War times when telegraphers tapped "XXX" to end transmissions. The Roman numeral "XXX" stands for the number 30, so it was transformed into "-30-" for modern printing usage. Today, the more modern and accepted use is "###" to signal the end of the release. This small gesture is a valuable mental note to those who are reading your release; it simply states that you are done and now they can decide if you are ready to get booked.

Final Quick National Network Attracting Press Release Tips:

- Make your press release *no longer than one page*.

- *Start strong*; grab the reader's attention with your headline and first paragraph.

- Use a *matter-of-fact tone* and avoid flowery words and too many adjectives at all costs.

- Use *strong verbs* to cut down on extra adjective use.

- *Avoid the hype.* Your press release should never have a need for exclamation points!!!

- Send the release to editors that directly *cover your field* & that have interest in your expertise.

- Use *active*, not passive, voice.

- *Be clear, concise, and complete.*

- Give the complete facts in as few words as possible

- Make sure the release addresses real news and is not an advertisement for you or your brand.

- Proofread, proofread, proofread.

- Oh...and *KEEP IT SIMPLE STUPID*!

Do the work in your industry, gain the expertise and knowledge first. Once the work is done, use the guidelines we've provided to gain national network attention. Before you know it, you, your message, and your brand will be booked and seen (or heard) by millions across the nation and hopefully, around the world.

CRYSTAL I. BERGER

Crystal I. Berger is an award-winning journalist and the Co-Founder and CEO of Pinnacle Media Corporation. She is dedicated to breaking the barriers to entry in media via the use of smart technology. Crystal advocates that shifting the mindset is key to both personal and professional breakthroughs. Her SHIFT Philosophy can take anyone from the ordinary to the extraordinary in any area of life. Crystal is a nationally recognized network producer and writer. She writes regularly for Black Enterprise, Mediabistro, and FOX News Opinions. Crystal's book, "Be Extraordinary: Claiming a Life of Purpose, Passion and Prosperity" explores why and how embracing individual uniqueness can propel anyone to a life of personal and professional significance.

www.getreadygetsetgetbooked.com
www.instagram.com/cbinspires
www.facebook.com/crystaliberger
www.soundcloud.com/crystalberger

YOUR BRAND WALKS ON STAGE BEFORE YOU DO!

HOW TO CREATE A STRONG BRAND IDENTITY

MARSHALL FOX

Your reputation precedes you. This has never been truer than today. Every time you speak, it is your brand that opens for you. Your brand unabashedly marches right up those steps and clear across the stage before you even pick up the microphone. It decides whether your audience will be excitedly anticipating what you have to say or skeptically dreading it. In today's world that seems like it revolves around social media, if you do not proactively build and manage your personal brand, it will take on a life of its own.

Take the time to really dive into the elements outlined in this chapter. By the time you have read this chapter, answered the questions, and studied your answers, you will have a clearly defined foundation upon which to manage your personal brand.

What exactly is a personal brand? Before we get into exactly what your personal brand consists of, it is important to know what your brand is NOT. It is *not* your logo. It is not your website. It is not your speaker press kit, your business cards, or your social media presence. Your brand is none of these

things alone, but all of these things combined *and more.*
Your brand is who the market thinks you are, not who *you*
think you are or who they *tell* you they think you are. It is
who they tell *other people* they think you are.

YOUR BRAND *IS* YOU

*"All of us need to understand the importance of branding.
We are CEOs of our own companies: Me, Inc. To be in
business today, our most important job is to be head
marketer for the brand called: YOU."*
Tom Peters, Fast Company

How do I build my personal brand?

PART 1: The Core

Building a personal brand requires a deep level of self-
discovery. It starts at your core and consists of 3 main
elements: self, vision, and message. Use the questions below
to clearly define your brand core. By taking the time to
answer these questions honestly, you will be setting your
brand up for success while minimizing the risk of nasty
surprises. **Do not move on to the next section without
answering each of these questions thoroughly.**

**Brand Core Element #1: Define Yourself (Self-
Assessment)**

- *Who are you?*
- *What is your purpose?*

- *What do you feel you were put on this Earth to accomplish?*

- *What are your values?*

- *What is your "Why?"*

Brand Core Element #2: Define Your Vision

- *What is your mission?*

- *Why did you decide to be a speaker?*

- *What do you want to achieve in your speaking career?*

- *What do you want to have accomplished in 10 years?*

- *What legacy do you want to leave behind?*

Brand Core Element #3: Define Your Message

This is not so much about *what* you should be sharing, but *how* you should be sharing it. But if you need a quick pointer on *what*, your messaging should revolve around your values, your strengths, your mission, and your gift.

VALUES + STRENGTHS + MISSION + GIFT = MESSAGE

It is important to keep in mind that your message is not only shared when you are behind a microphone, but it is also being conveyed constantly. It is emitting at all times like a radar signal. There is no off-switch; when you are speaking on stage, when networking, at events, church, work, on social media, and even in your head. In fact, your self-talk is just as important as your external communication. Your internal messaging comes through externally whether you realize it or not.

It is critical that your messaging is consistent across all of your touch points: website, social media, email, in-person communication, etc. With everything that you post, ask yourself "Does this speak to my tribe?" Is who you are *without* the microphone who you are *behind* the microphone? Does your *online* persona align with your *offline* persona?

Once your core is identified, take it a step further to identify your market.

Part 2: The Market

Clearly defining your market is the second key step in the foundation of your personal brand. Who you speak to makes up a large part of your brand identity. Not just in speaking, but in business. Here are some examples:

Black Speakers Network --- As you may have noticed, a large part of this group's identity is in the name: Black Speakers. By focusing on this niche, it is easier for BSN to attract speakers, grow their brand recognition and ultimately, identity. Without this niche as clearly defined BSN's identity would be vague and unfocused.

120 Design Studio -- Graphic Design for Speakers. As a graphic design studio that primarily serves Speakers, Authors, Coaches, and Consultants, we have quickly become the go-to agency for that niche. How? Simply by *focusing* on that market. As we grow our clientele, we are able to:

- Receive referrals from our speaker clients of other speakers
- Start to identify specific pain points

Compiling this data over time allows us to refine our service and messaging which **deepens our impact in this market.** This is applicable as a speaker.

By clearly defining your audience, you are able to:

- Connect right to that person/avatar, a stronger connection
- Be considered a subject matter expert to your specific audience
- Focus on that specific audience's needs and pain points
- Have a clear lane and focus

"I see people dig too many shallow holes and then wonder why they never strike oil."
Darren Hardy

DEFINE YOUR AUDIENCE

Ask yourself the following questions to help define your market:

Who do you speak to?

Who are your most loyal supporters?

Who most values your expertise and gift?

What do others come to you for advice about?

What types of people are booking you or buying your products and services?

Go Deeper: DEFINE YOUR DEMOGRAPHIC

- *What are the **values** of your target market?*

- *What kind of **lifestyle** do they lead?*

- *What **problems** do they tend to have that you can solve through your message, products and services?*

- ***Where are they** and how can you reach them? Social media?*

- *Is your **speaking fee structure** in alignment with your target market?*

WHO ARE YOUR COMPETITORS?

As a Speaker, you may not have direct *competitors*, but you should still know who the major players are in your space. Be nosey! Google your niche (Ex. Best Youth Motivational Speakers). Check out their websites and social media accounts and take notes!

- *Who are they?*

- *What are they doing well as it relates to their online presence and visual brand identity?*

- *What do not they not do well that you can do better?*

When your core and your market are clearly identified, you will have a good handle on your personal brand and begin to expand it.

How do I *expand* my personal brand?

If you want to reach more people and impact more lives, you have to make sure your message falls in the blast radius of what people are looking for (or vice versa).

- **Build Brand Recognition**
  - **High Quality Design**
    - Here are a few design essentials you should have as a professional speaker: Personal Brand Logo, Speaker Website, Speaker Sheet, Book Covers, Business Cards, Social Media Graphics and Flyers
    - Every design decision that is made should quickly and easily resonate with your target audience. If you have a design that you love but it completely flies over the head of your target audience, it may miss the mark, sending a message that you did not intend.
    - Your designer should take the time to understand you, your message, your vision, and overall business: You should partner with a designer that is **Consistent**, **High Quality**, **Accessible***, and **Understands Your Needs**

- Make sure all designs are: Simple, Memorable, Timeless, Versatile, and Appropriate.

- *Have a backup plan. If you have a really good designer, there will likely be times when they are booked solid. Have a high-quality Plan B ready. Good designers should be able to refer you to someone in their network should they be unavailable

- ○ **Create a Design Language that is Your Own**

  - Have a consistent look and feel across all of your touch points based on your visual brand identity

  - What is your signature style? Whether it be your design, your message, or your wardrobe, create one and stick to it.

- ○ **Ensure Quality is Consistent**

  - If you do not have one team working on your designs, make sure you always get the source files and color codes from your designer. This allows the next designer to easily make changes and match colors

How do I *manage* my personal brand?

This one is simple. ***Be who you say you are.*** Your persona should be the same whether you are online or offline. Make sure your messaging is consistent across platforms and appropriate for your audience. Be sure to let your personality shine through. In all interactions, make sure you stick to your core values. Are you partnering with people and brands who are in alignment with you, your values, and your message? If not, do not be afraid to turn a deal or a gig down if it is not in alignment with who you are and what you stand for. This can be difficult, especially when you are in desperate need of "that check" but failing to stick to this rule can be detrimental to your brand.

By answering the questions outlined in this chapter, you should have a thorough understanding of:

- What a personal brand is
- What is needed to start building it
- How to expand your personal brand
- How to manage it

This is not intended to be a deep, detailed process. Consider this a simple starting point. If you would like detailed information about what design elements are essential to building your personal brand, visit www.120designstudio.com and download our FREE Ultimate Speaker Brand Design Checklist. Keep this in mind: If you are not actively building, expanding, and managing your brand, you are tearing it down.

MARSHALL FOX

 Marshall is a graphic designer, brand consultant, and CEO of 120 Design Studio, LLC, one of the highest-rated graphic design agencies in the United States. His agency specializes in helping authors, speakers, coaches, and solopreneurs in two major areas where they consistently fall short: their visual brand identity and online presence. His keen sense of design and attention to detail helps his clients increase brand awareness, credibility, and sales.

In less than three years, Marshall has entered the graphic design space, helped over 300 clients, and has built 120 Design Studio into a six-figure agency. Marshall and his team enjoy helping their clients ensure the quality of their visual brand matches the quality of their services, products, and other offerings. When Marshall is not sipping coffee and obsessing over color palettes, he's spending time with his wife and four children.

www.120designstudio.com
www.facebook.com/120designstudio
www.instagram.com/120designstudio
www.instagram.com/marshallfox
www.linkedin.com/company/120-design-studio

#CALLFORSPEAKERS

HOW TO MAKE YOUR SPEAKER PROPOSAL STAND OUT

AURORA GREGORY

Standing out is defined as someone or something being remarkably superior to others. The quality of standing out is one of those intangible character traits that is unmistakable when you see it. And it is that unmistakable quality that meeting, conference and event planners are looking for when selecting speakers to put in front of their audiences.

Your speaker proposal has to entice meeting and conference planners to want to hear what you have to say before you ever take the stage. This is where you make the case for why you should be on an event's agenda and why their audience would be interested in listening to you. Your speaker proposal has to stand out by being distinctively different, so you do not blend in with all of the other speakers vying for the stage. You need to create your proposal in a way that screams "I am the speaker you have been looking for!"

A speaker proposal is the place where you lay out the promise for what you will deliver from the stage. To get selected, you have to do more than just list your talking points. You have to sell your topic, sell your expertise, sell your enthusiasm – all while making a compelling argument for why this session is one that attendees simply will not want to miss. One of the keys to a winning proposal is writing your copy with some creativity and a bit of drama.

Why Great Writing Wins The Race

It is important to remember when you are submitting a proposal to speak at an event, you are entering a competition. Yours may be one of dozens, if not hundreds of speaker proposals, so getting on the agenda will not be easy. Your job is to make it as difficult as possible for a conference planner to pass on your presentation. Your ultimate goal is to win, which is why your proposal has to be written with a bit of sparkle and flair.

Every conference or event is in the business of putting the best speakers and the most interesting presentations in front of their audience. Your proposal must demonstrate you will be a great addition to the conference festivities, theme, goals and/or objectives. This is your opportunity to express how compelling you will be on stage. The first step in that process is to create a powerful proposal that engages the reader. If you do not take the time to put together a compelling, thought-provoking, and inspiring proposal, why should an event planner have faith you will be able to deliver from the stage?

Making Magic At The Keyboard

The first step in creating a stand-out speaker proposal is to pick a topic that resonates with the audience. No amount of creative writing can "sell" a presentation that does not connect with its intended target. And worst of all, if you do manage to get selected, you run the risk of being a disappointment once you hit the stage.

Picking a hot topic is imperative. What is a hot topic? Something that inspires, generates buzz, a new innovation, or a future trend. Talk to friends and colleagues to brainstorm about what other people are interested in and talking about in the subject area you speak about. Do a little web searching to find out what is trending and what is on the minds of other thought-leaders.

Some examples of hot topics might be a discussion about the latest efforts to empower women in the workplace or encouraging confidence in girls to pursue careers in male-dominated professions. A talk about the creative application of business innovation trends for entrepreneurs or a motivational speech on creating an adaptable workforce to meet dynamic business demands are also examples of hot topics. Today's renewed focus on the connection between nutrition and quality of life or the growing use of artificial intelligence (AI) in business applications are a few more. Find out what is hot in your area of expertise and build your proposal around that topic.

Conversely, you want to stay away from topics that are clearly retreads. Anything that has been around for years or is an established practice, should be avoided. Unless you are bringing a really fresh spin or a complete reinvention of something tried and true, you will want to steer clear of anything that might be perceived as mundane or pedestrian.

It is important to remember, not only does your talk have to wow the selection committee, it has to be highly attractive to conference attendees. Organizers want their program to be chockful of scintillating talks and "cannot miss" topics, so they can fill the seats.

Bring Some Flair To Your Title – That is Where the Sales Job Starts

The old expression "always put your best forward" certainly applies when it comes to your proposal. The first thing the selection committee will see is your title. It might be a small amount of copy, but these few words might be the most important you write. This is the hook that lures in the reader. Be sure to take time with your title. A perfect title can be the difference between success and failure.

A killer title demands attention, sets the stage for the presentation, whets the reader's appetite and, when possible, creates intrigue. A clever turn of a phrase, double entendre, catchy play on words, or pop-culture reference can amp up interest in your session. A good title describes what the reader can expect, while a great title tells them what they will learn in an intriguing way. A great title will also build drama, while communicating what the presentation will cover. Remember, being clever just for clever's sake will not help you get selected if your title does not actually describe what the session is about. It is important that a title be impactful, compelling, concise, and most of all – on point!

Unleash Your Inner Storyteller

When developing your proposal, you will want to think about how you can transform it into a story – one that has a thought-provoking opening/dilemma, a "damn-the-torpedoes" middle, and a hard-fought victorious ending. A good story connects to an emotion, which in turn creates more of a lasting impression than straight up facts and figures. (Not to say that you should not include a choice stat or two, if they support the power of your story.)

Creating a story is actually simpler than you might think. Start with the problem or existing trend, explain how obstacles were overcome, and then wrap up with the impact/achievement or what your audience will be empowered to do after listening to you. It might be helpful to think of the description of your speech as a movie trailer that teases great things to come.

It is also important to keep in mind that deftly turning your proposal into a story demonstrates to the event and conference planners that your presentation will also be well worth the journey and clearly worthy of selection for their event.

Weak Words Are Kryptonite – Use Power Words To Amp Up The Interest

The words you choose for your proposal are important. And because you most likely are going to be limited in how many you can use, it is critical to select them wisely. Weak words in a speaker proposal subliminally communicate a weak speaker and a weak presentation. What are weak words? These are passive words, which are often seen as vague, lacking specificity, unnecessary, and not particularly confident. Examples include really, nice, cool, interesting, almost, fairly, etc.

Conversely, strong, or positive words will make the reader feel something. These might include absolutely, acclaimed, daring, eye-opening, ingenious, lucrative, powerful, etc. Obviously, it is important not to overuse such words, but a few strategically sprinkled throughout your proposal can go a long way toward strengthening your prose, adding punch, and helping you get selected to speak.

To the Victor Goes the Spoils

The simple reality is that there are a lot of great speakers out there. Many apply to speak at events, but few are chosen. In the case of TED Talks, conference curators consider about 10,000 application submissions to select approximately 65 slots for the main stage. That is pretty stiff competition.

This is why it is important to increase your chances of getting picked by using engaging, persuasive language to draw event planners to your proposal. Push past your comfort zone and talk about yourself and your presentation in glowing, engaging, charismatic terms and you will stand head and shoulders above the crowd to land more of the stages you pitch.

#

Aurora Gregory is a business marketing and communications coach for financial service companies and entrepreneurs. She is the co-author of Get Picked: Tips, Tricks, And Tools for Creating An Irresistible Speaker Proposal and is a regular speaker on growing revenue through marketing and using public speaking to build a career, grow a business or spread a message. Learn more at www.AuroraGregory.com.

Aurora Gregory

Marketer. Coach. Author. Speaker.

As an eighth grader, Aurora was a finalist in a speech contest. She did not win, but that just might have been the start of her career as a communicator. Some of the biggest brands in business have worked with her to get their message right and create marketing communications strategies that connect with target audiences and deliver great outcomes. Aurora is a business marketing and communications coach for financial services companies and entrepreneurs. She is the co-author of Get Picked: Tips, Tricks, and Tools For An Irresistible Speaker Proposal. A regular speaker on growing revenue through marketing and using public speaking to build a career, grow a business or spread a message, nothing delights her more than helping clients solve problems that deliver big results. When she's not talking, you will likely find Aurora hiking the foothills in her hometown or on her sofa watching classic movies.

www.auroragregory.com
www.facebook.com/AuroraGregoryBiz
Instagram.com/aurora_gregory
www.linkedin.com/in/auroragregory

ARE BORING BIOS BLOCKING YOUR BOOKINGS?

HOW TO CRAFT A WINNING SPEAKER BIO

TIERANY GRIFFIN

You get "the" email.

You know the one that confirms you have been chosen for that major speaking opportunity that you have been seeking, waiting, and praying for! Following the confirmation paragraph, you read: "Please reply with your professional bio and headshot and we will send a follow-up email with additional instructions."

Then it hits – YOU DO NOT HAVE A PROFESSIONAL BIO! Or worse – It is boring.

Now I know the term "boring" is subjective, however, when it comes to your professional bio, the purpose is not only to highlight your skills and expertise but to also serve as a marketing tool to promote your brand. It not only introduces your audience to you and your offerings, but it allows them to catch a glimpse into what to expect when they encounter your brand.

Think of it this way – have you ever experienced food that was visually appealing, but the taste was not there, almost like the seasoning was missing? Or maybe it was seasoned but something was missing? Well, that is the difference between a professional bio and a CAPTIVATING professional bio. It is the "special seasoning" that makes your brand delectable to your customer's palate!

Writing a captivating bio can seem like a daunting task, but it may not be as difficult as you think. Here are my top 5 keys to crafting an amazing speaker's bio.

1. K.I.S. Your Bio

One of the major keys to creating a captivating bio is "K.I.S." – *Keep It Succinct*. Short and concise is the way to go when it comes to writing a compelling bio. Even so, thanks to technology, humans are now experiencing the shortest attention span EVER (around 8 seconds) so if you do not capture your reader's attention quickly, your hard work is falling on deaf ears. The industry standard is around 200 words, but if you can hit all your marks in 150-words or less, you will be a bio superstar. Anything over, you may just be kissing your readers (and golden opportunities!) goodbye.

2. Brag, Don't Drag

Piggybacking off the first point, it is important to be very selective of the information that is shared in a captivating bio. It is safe to say that no matter how much experience or longevity, no one wants to read your entire journey, moment by moment. Pick 2-3 career highlights (preferably most recent) and build on those. We all know it was a very special moment but receiving that award in 2nd grade should not be mentioned in your professional bio. Also, be careful with descriptive words. If used incorrectly, you can come off a bit cavalier, not to mention they can eat up your word count.

3. Think in Third

Another major key to creating a winning speaker's bio is to "Think in Third" – third person, that is. A common mistake that most make is they either write from a first-person perspective or they use all three persons in one bio. It is standard and professional to either write in the third person, referring to yourself as "he"/" she" (I know it sounds weird, but trust me it is worth it!) or by name. This enables a more polished tone to your bio and the repetition of your name helps readers remember exactly who you are.

4. Just A Touch... Of Personality

If I had to declare the most important key to a winning bio, it would be this one. In a bio, personality is power. Here is the thing: you must be careful how you use it. Too much personality can be distracting, whereas too little can be mind-numbing. It is your job to find a happy medium. I refer to it as the "first note" effect. Just like a singer, if the bio starts off on the right first note, it captivates your audience and holds them for the duration of the story. On the other hand, if things start off amiss or dry, it changes the dynamics and alters the reader's experience.

Steering clear of off-color jokes and puns, a great way to infuse personality is by opening with a witty quote or byline. This sets the tone for what is to come in your bio and connect the story to something relatable. If you would prefer a cleverer approach, you could adopt the "Show, don't tell" method. This idiom declares that whenever possible do not tell someone who you are, show them. For example, instead of telling you "I am a writer who specializes in professional biographies and content management" in my first sentence, I would write something like "As Suite Spot Communications Boutique's Executive Creator, Tierany does more than write stories and wrangle content all day." See what I did there?

5. *Say Your Name, Say Your Name*

Now I know you are thinking "Tierany, why in the world would I not write my name in my own bio?" And my response would be "Trust me. It happens."

I cannot count the number of times that I have been sent bios to review or update and the first sentence is "Joe has been a professional speaker for x number of years. He has spoken here, there and everywhere." First, Joe who? And is Joe his professional name or something that his family and friends call him? Either way, this is a negative. Always remember - when stating your name in your bio, always refer to your professional name. Nicknames, social media handles, or personal monikers are a no-no! You are a professional and your bio should reflect as such. And as much as we love "Peaches" or "Champ" at the family reunion, we do not need to hear about them when you are introduced as a professional speaker to the masses.

Now that you have the keys to the winning bio kingdom, you will have no issues crafting a bio that is impactful, impressive, and - perhaps most importantly – interesting. As you continue to develop, revisit your work, and keep refining and refreshing your bio, at least every six months. That way, when you get "the" email you will not have to get ready – you will stay ready.

TIERANY GRIFFIN

Armed with an indelible love for bringing stories to life, Tierany Griffin-Purdie is a creative "Jill-of-all-trades" who has spent most of her life writing short, fictional stories, reading every book she could get her hands on, and exploring her love for music and style.

An eight-year blogging veteran, content strategist and executive creative, Tierany continues to thrive at the intersection of communication, digital media, and style. She's worked with numerous clients including Human Rights Campaign, America's largest civil rights organization working to achieve lesbian, gay, bisexual, transgender and queer equality and Southern Noir Weddings, a resource of southern inspiration for brides of color.

Tierany is a speaker, host and correspondent who leverages her background in style, communications, and media to cultivate a community of excellence and welcomes opportunities to collaborate and connect with other exceptional women.

www.workwithtierany.com
www.facebook.com/businessissuite
www.instagram.com/businessisuite

I WROTE MY BOOK, NOW WHAT?

HOW TO BECOME A BEST-SELLING AUTHOR

MWALE AND CHANTEL HENRY

The hallmark of every great speaker is an equally inspiring business card. No, I am not talking about a business card in the traditional sense. The 21st-century business card is about 5 x 8 inches, 110 pages, and around 20,000 words. If you have not yet figured out what I mean, let me be clear, the best business card you can have is a book. While some would challenge my theory with rebuttals such as: 'I do not need a book, people do not read as much as they used to,' or I have multiple businesses a book just wouldn't capture everything.' As a publisher of dozens of international bestselling books, I have heard practically every excuse you can think of from speakers who unknowingly are setting themselves up to be just ordinary. Thankfully many of you reading this would have already broken that glass ceiling and are now on a journey to become extraordinary.

The path to having extraordinary success as a speaker is solidifying yourself as not just an author but an international bestselling author. As such, you join the ranks of great orators like Lisa Nichols, T.D. Jakes, Barak Obama, and Les Brown, to name a few. These men and women represent speakers who are not only committed to their craft but are widely received by the public they serve. Their best seller status demonstrates that they have done the work and thousands of people are eagerly consuming their content. While you may not have the name recognition of those leaders, you do have a unique services proposition that can catapult you to the top of any bestsellers list.

Discovering and Applying Your USP

Your Unique Service Proposition (USP) is defined by two elements of your story - Pain and Purpose. Have you ever noticed how some of your peers just seem to have the Midas Touch? Everything they touch turns to gold whenever they launch a new product or program, you will see them shortly after, celebrating how many people signed up for the offer.

One of the reasons we are so committed to helping coaches and speakers excel in their business is because we remember a time when all we wanted was an opportunity.

We would spend hours cold calling colleges and universities to pitch ourselves for their events. If we did not hear, "not at this time," we heard "send us an email and we will get back to you." It was not long before disappointment and defeat set in as we sunk down into our office chairs feeling the weight of our calling pushing us down like a ton of bricks. I would sit in that chair for hours trying to build up enough courage to go at it again.

Then I remembered a lesson my mentor told me years earlier: "People do not care how much you know until they know how much you care."

Speak Up!

We failed to book engagements because we were pitching our knowledge, not our Why.

Yes, the universities appreciated us having bachelors and master's degrees, but they were not impressed.

There were plenty of other speakers who had the same thing or even fewer qualifications. What transformed their minds and why I am able to get paid to speak all over the world is when I told them that despite being an international bestselling author, a college professor and someone who has traveled to 11 countries by the time I was 21 years old, there was a time when merely surviving was considered success.

Growing up in Baltimore and having a father addicted to drugs I knew education was my ticket to freedom.

I was one of the first in my family to attend college and the only one to obtain a master's degree.

The transparency that I shared about my pain made them appreciate my expertise more. People do not care how much you know until they know how much and WHY you care.

To be a highly paid speaker and international bestselling author, your story and brand must reveal your pain. Think about a painful experience (that you have healed from) that you can use to accelerate your business, ask yourself the following questions:

1. What is something painful that has happened to me and I do not mind sharing with the world?

2. What major lessons have I learned from that experience?

3. Why does that experience make me passionate about the products and services that I offer in my business?

When you are recalling your pain points, sometimes, your stories may be hidden as moments or incidents. Do not think it is some grand, twist and turn narration of a Terry McMillan novel.

Catalog your moments, the drive to work, the accident you witnessed, the dreaded phone call you received, the moment you saw the eviction notice on your door, the moment your doctor called you into their office to talk about your lab results, your foreclosure notice, the list goes on.

While writing your story, show me the texture of each millisecond, invite me to sit next to you during your doctor's appointment, describe the scene, the taste, color, sound, mood, etc.

People want to know you, your journey, your scars. This transparency develops trust from your readers and makes them rally behind your work. They do the marketing for you which is a key step in becoming a bestseller.

Speak Up!

The next P in our triple P formula takes your Why to another level. It is all about communicating your purpose.

If we were to ask you 3 reasons why you are a speaker, would you be able to communicate your why in such a way that it makes your audience cry?

People are moved to buy from their emotions as much as they are prompted to buy from their convictions. Think about the last time you bought a vitamin or dietary supplement.

Chances are you saw a before and after picture of the person promoting the product and it was so emotionally riveting for you that it caused you to press the buy button on the screen.

Maybe you thought about how you would be perceived by the opposite sex or how nice you would look in those jeans without the extra pounds.

Paint such a vivid picture for your audience about why you believe in your mission and why they should too. This act of communication will help them to choose you every time.

When your audience has made the choice to buy into you, your pain and purpose, then you can truly make a profit.

The Ultimate Status Symbol

Being a bestselling author is a highly respected and coveted title. It shows the world that more than just your mom and dad care about your work. It is therefore essential to apply the Triple P Formula (Pain, Purpose, Profit) to increase your chances of hitting the bestsellers list. When those bases are covered, it is easy to market your book in such a way that people buy it when you launch. Amazon, for example, allows authors to hit number one in multiple categories as long as they have the sales to back it up. Unlike the New York Times Bestsellers List, you do not need 3,000 or more sales in a 24-hour period to be an Amazon Bestseller. Depending on your book's category, 1-50 sales within a day will help you land the top spot.

I have even seen a case where simply placing a client's book in a non-competitive category allowed them to rank as number one because there were no other books released on that day (within the same genre). While many of you may be in "do-it-yourself" mode I do not recommend attempting the self-publishing journey by yourself especially if you want to become a bestselling author.

The chances of you ranking in a category are much higher when you have proven research for which categories are the least competitive and when you have done the proper work in advance (applying the Triple P Formula) to grow your community of supporters to purchase your book on launch day. When those elements are aligned, you will enjoy a lasting brand and solidify yourself as an international bestselling author.

Mwale and Chantel Henry

Mwale and Chantel Henry are highly requested speakers and transformational coaches. Affectionately known as the millennial power couple, this dynamic duo maintains a global presence impacting lives through ministry and non-profit work with at risk-youth in Trinidad and Tobago. As owners of the Legacy Project, based in Atlanta, Georgia, Mwale & Chantel are on a mission to help 1,000 people become international bestselling authors by 2020.

For more information visit www.ourlegacyproject.org

www.thebestsellersacademy.com
www.Facebook.com/MwaleandChantel

WHY SHOULD I CALL YOU BACK?

THE ART OF PITCHING TO THE MEDIA

CANDICE NICOLE

No, this is not about pitching in baseball ladies and gentlemen (HaHa). We are going to discuss how to pitch the perfect pitch to secure you media. A pitch (in the form of an email) is a suggested story idea that is sent to media outlets (radio/tv/digital/bloggers/journalists). The pitch provides more information to the individual about the idea/person you are reaching out to them about. Why is this important as a Speaker? It shows that you are a credible source in your craft, it will create a platform for you to be seen as an expert, and more.

Before I go into more detail of how to craft your pitch, how to locate media contacts, the follow-up process, and the actual securing of media placement, I want to provide a breakdown of the prep that should happen before the execution. This part is very important because it gives you time to plan, which is very important in any task you want to achieve.

How do you prep and plan before you begin to pitch? See below for my checklist on the items that are needed.

- **Info One Sheet or EPK (Electronic Press Kit)** - This will provide the media outlet instant information in one controlled area about you

- **Pitch Angles** - These will be the story ideas that you have crafted and would like to discuss with the media outlet. Always strive to create 5-7 that you can circulate to different media outlets

- **Professional Headshot** – Choose High-Resolution images that can be used for promoting your appearance

- **Social Media/Website/Info Page** - You want to make sure your Social Media is updated and when individuals visit, they know exactly what you do. Your Social Media should represent your brand. The same for your Website/Info Page. Make sure you are highlighting the correct sections you want individuals to visit on your Website/Info Page

- **Video Footage/Images** - This is not always needed, but if you have video footage of yourself speaking or images of you addressing a crowd, it is a plus

- **Knowledge of Schedule** - This is very important. Media outlets are constantly being pitched to, so when they respond with a date in mind, you want to be sure you know your schedule. If you do not have flexibility with your schedule, provide some days/times that you would be available and hopefully it will fit with their availability.

Alright! Now, that we have the checklist mapped out, we can shift to the actual art of pitching. Pitching is very tedious and a task that causes individuals to showcase patience, but also something that can be very rewarding when you begin securing the media placements that you desire. It will not happen overnight, and you must not take anything personal. If a media outlet does not respond, there are a variety of reasons why they have not. Below, you will find a breakdown of what to include, what not include, and how to personalize your pitch.

What to put in your Media Pitch

- An introduction of who you are

- Information on why you are reaching out to them

- Reference something you have seen them cover in the past (suggesting that is why that certain media outlet is a match for a feature)

- Various pitch angles

- Date (If pitching an event or conference you are planning or participating in)

- Links (if wanting to send any images/videos)

What to NOT put in your Media Pitch

- Attachments

- Not having a greeting

- Not having a proper email subject

Speak Up!

- No in-depth information on why you are reaching out to them

- One pitch suggestion

- Pressure to interview

How to make your Pitch Personal

- Research the journalist/reporter

- Greet them by their name (if available)

- Refer to an article they recently wrote

- Prior to the pitch, send an email inquiring about what they write about (this can be also known as an intro email)

Next, you will need to seek out media contacts at the media outlets you are interested in securing. I have created a list of how this can assist you because this process alone may be intimidating if you have never interacted with media before.

- Research (Social Media/Digital Platforms)

- Follow publicists and pay attention to who they thank for interviewing their clients - You can locate publicists by searching hashtags #PR #Publicist and also entering "Publicist" into the search field on any Social Media platforms

- Cision & Meltwater (Paid Service)

- HARO (Help a Reporter Out) *FREE Service*

- Networking with Journalists (Attend Meetups/Conferences)

- Cold Calling (It still works and sometimes is the fastest way to locate the correct contact)

As you begin to create your media contacts, you will want to create an online database so that you can easily access your contact list when you are pitching. I am a huge fan of utilizing services that will not break the bank because as you know, monthly payments can start to add up over time. I use Google Sheets. Why Google Sheets? It is FREE and I can have access to my list via my computer and the app on my phone. If I am traveling, do not have access to my laptop, and need to issue an email or pitch; I can still access my lists.

BONUS Make sure you categorize your lists. Some examples of column labels are media outlet, name of contact, email, date pitch was issued, medium (tv/radio/digital) and response (yes, no or passed).

A major tip that will assist you with pitching yourself is staying on top of current events, upcoming holidays, and trends. For example, if you are a relationship expert and see that there has been a decrease in divorces, that may be a great opportunity to pitch yourself to your local media on sharing your thoughts on why this has occurred.

Your follow-up is a very important component of your pitching strategy. Personally, I will send 3-4 follow-ups to a media outlet before I table that specific pitch. As I say table the pitch, I do not mean that I will not ever reach out to that media outlet again, but I will reach out in another 30-60 days and sometimes with a new set of pitch angles.

As you can see, there is a lot of planning and prepping when it comes to The Art of Pitching the Media, but if you spend time planning and organizing, you will create your own system to handle your pitches. Wishing all of you the best in your pitch process! Remember, it will not happen overnight, and your patience will be tested, but the reward will make it worth the sacrifice. Happy Pitching!

BONUS: As this chapter has been dedicated to pitching, I thought that it would be helpful to provide you with a pitch template so you can see an actual layout and verbiage I have used to secure TV placements for clients. To download your FREE pitch template, please visit www.bit.ly/bsnspeakuppitchtemplate.

CANDICE NICOLE

 A graduate from Morgan State University with a degree in Communications, concentration Public Relations, Candice Nicole is a true lover of PR! From interning in LA at Von Dutch Originals to handling Spike Lee's "Red Hook Summer" DC press tour and movie screening, she is a well-rounded Publicist that keeps growing each year in her career.

CNPR clients have been featured on BET, TV One, STEVE, The TODAY Show, MSNBC, Essence, SHEEN Magazine, Rolling Out, The Huff Post, Black Enterprise, Local/Regional TV, Radio & More.

Candice is an Award-Winning Publicist, listed as Top 25 African American Publicists in The Huff Post and is dedicated to crafting compelling stories of CNPR clients.

www.bit.ly/connectwithcnpr
www.twitter.com/CandiceNicolePR
www.instagram.com/CandiceNicolePR
www.linkedin.com/in/candicenicolepr

FIND YOUR STAGE!

BUILDING A STRATEGY TO STAY CONSISTENTLY BOOKED

BRIAN J. OLDS

Congratulations! You have been selected as our keynote speaker!

How often would you like to wake up to an email with that subject line? It is possible for you regardless of where you are in your professional speaker journey. All it takes is adopting a few new habits combined with a shift in mindset. In my opinion, too many speakers are focused on chasing engagements as opposed to building a strategy that will produce a steady stream of speaking opportunities.

Before we dive in, there are a few Find Your Stage™ principles that we need to cover to address the mindset of a successful professional speaker.

Find Your Stage Principle 1: This is a long-term relationship-based business. I recently conducted a speaking engagement for the Baltimore professional chapter of the National Society of Black Engineers. My first time speaking for this group was over five years ago. How did I hear about both opportunities? Relationships. The same member referred me to this engagement both times. The first time I spoke to the group he was a new member. Fast forward five years later, he is now the president of the chapter. The work you are doing now may not show up until years later, but if you are only focused on getting booked now, you will miss those opportunities.

Find Your Stage Principle 2: Stop expecting to be paid a "speaking fee" for every speaking engagement. There are several chapters in this book that emphasize the importance of developing multiple streams of income as a speaker. The process of doing so is beyond the scope of this chapter, however, just in case it has not been drilled into your mind yet, it is worth restating. To be successful in this business, you need to create and sell products or services that serve your audience outside of your presentation. If you do not have this yet, you are leaving money on the table every time you speak.

Find Your Stage Principle 3: You are solely responsible for booking yourself to speak. I am a member of several online speaking communities including the one we have for Black Speakers Network. Whenever we ask speakers about the #1 challenge they struggle with, the answer is always finding more PAID speaking engagements. While this may be true on the surface, it still makes me laugh when I hear new speakers say things like:

- "I am going to hire a speaker's agent to book all of my engagements."
- "I am going to sign up for a speakers bureau."

- "I am going to hire a virtual assistant to handle all my bookings for me."

It is not that these options are inherently wrong. As a speaker, you should tap into as many resources as possible to get access to the audience that you serve. The fundamental challenge with the statements above is that often speakers who make these statements are not looking to supplement their booking efforts, but rather replace them.

Action Item: Wherever you are as you read this, I want you to say this statement out loud to yourself five times: **I (SAY YOUR NAME), AM SOLELY RESPONSIBLE FOR BOOKING MYSELF TO SPEAK**. You, your presentation, and the solutions you create for your audience are the best marketing tools at your disposal.

Now that we have these basic principles in mind, let's talk about how to stay consistently booked. Do you need to book more speaking engagements? Yes. But more important than booking your next engagement is creating a purposeful plan and process to speak. Your process must consider a few essential elements. I call this the **B.S.N. Model™ for Building A Strategy to Stay Consistently Booked.**

Element One: Build Your List

"The richest people in the world build networks; everyone else looks for work," stated Robert Kiyosaki. Your success, as well as your compensation as a speaker, are determined by two factors: The number of people you serve and the amount of value you consistently deliver to your audience. If you want to increase your income, you have two options.

Option 1 is to improve your influence and provide your unique gifts to a higher number of people than you currently impact.

Option 2 is to increase the amount of value you create for your audience by solving more significant problems or solving existing problems more efficiently.

Your list is one of the most critical elements of your marketing strategy. Many speakers fail to meet their speaking and revenue goals because they do not have a systematic way to create, organize and nurture a list that produces results. If you are speaking as a hobby then it is perfectly fine to wait for the phone to ring to book your next speaking engagement; however, professional speakers do not leave getting booked to luck. Instead, they have a focused intensity, backed up by a consistent action plan that will over time, lead to results.

Even if you are a new speaker with absolutely no speaking experience, you can build a list of at least 50 or more people who should be on your list. The reality is, the best speaker in the world cannot get booked to speak if nobody knows who you are or what you can do. The good news is that everyone has a list. It may be disorganized and fragmented across multiple places, but you have one.

ACTION ITEM: Grab a sheet of paper and take 30 minutes to complete the following questions - do not worry if you have contact information for these people yet. Just start with their names.

- How would you best describe your target audience?
- Who do you know in your target audience from the following connections:
  - Classmates (High School, College, Graduate School, Trade School)
  - Employment (current and past)
  - Places of worship
  - Social media connections (Facebook, Twitter, Instagram, Snapchat, LinkedIn)
  - Sports teams or social clubs
  - Fraternities or sororities
- What kinds of organizations and associations does your target market belong?
- Which organizations do you already have existing contacts?
- What professional trade conferences, events or seminars does your audience attend?
- What kind of podcasts does your audience listen to?
- Who are the influencers that your audience already trust and rely on for information?
- Who booked you for your last speaking opportunities?
- Where have other speakers in your niche spoken?

There are many more questions you can ask here, but with these questions, you can quickly build a solid starter list. Before you focus all your time and energy looking for speaking engagements from people you never met, why not start in your current circle of influence. **The people closest to you in your network should know three things:**

1. You are a speaker

2. Your area of expertise

3. You are actively speaking and looking for speaking engagements

Element Two: Segment Your List

Once you have your list, you will need to segment it into different categories based on your business relationship. Your goal as a speaker is to stay relevant and visible to the people who can either hire you (your clients), people who you serve (your audience), and people who can connect you to those people (influencers). Each of these segments will be expecting different kinds of content from you. You can have many list segments but here are some basic definitions to help you get started.

Leads - Decision makers who have the authority to book you to speak. These may include executives, HR leaders, or event planning committees. They make the final decision on who speaks and typically have full creative control over the entire event. These are the people you want to ensure your communication with is clear, concise, and timely. They are busy and likely under a lot of pressure to produce an event amidst a laundry list of other responsibilities.

Influencers - Individuals who cannot directly hire you to speak but can influence the decision of the people who do. This may include people who work in a company like executive assistants, managers, or support staff. While they may not be making the final decision, they can heavily influence who is selected to speak, so building and maintaining relationships with them is critical.

Current Clients - Anyone who has booked you to speak. I consider anyone a current client if I have an upcoming engagement or if I presented to their organization within the past 90 days. Make it a goal to be very easy to work with and to provide timely and clear communication. If your clients have a good experience with you, you are more likely to be rehired and referred.

Past Clients - Anyone who has booked you to speak previously but has not rehired you in the past 90 days. Sometimes, we get so focused on the next opportunity, we fail to stay in touch with the people who we have already built trust and demonstrated value. You should set a goal and track your rehire rate as a measure of your effectiveness as a speaker.

Audience - These are the people for whom you develop your presentation and solutions. This should be your largest list. Even though your client is the person hiring you to speak, your audience consists of the people you are ultimately accountable for serving. While your job as a speaker is to make your client happy, your more significant responsibility is to transform your audience.

Advocates – Your most loyal tribe. These people are a subsection of your audience who consistently purchase your products, attend your events, and freely share your content across social media and through word-of-mouth. You want to know who these people are and take GREAT care of them.

Element Three: Nurture Your List

Now that you realize the importance of building a list and segmenting, the natural next question should be; what do I do with the list? As we mentioned before, speaking is a long-term relationship-based business. You may be looking at your calendar of speaking engagements for the next three months and think that you are failing as a speaker. The reality is that your calendar of booked speaking engagements is not the only dashboard that matters. Your calendar of engagements is considered a lagging metric and one that you do not have 100% control over.

What you do have power over is how many people you are adding to your list, the frequency, and quality of your engagement, as well as your attitude throughout the process. You should be touching each segment of your list on a weekly basis to varying degrees. How you decide to break up your time will change based on your goals as a speaker. Your activity needs to match your goals. For instance, you cannot say you want to book ten speaking engagements per month, but your action reflects that you only submitted five proposals last month. You must make time and commit to nurturing your list every day.

Here are some dos and do not's as it relates to nurturing the relationships in your network.

Do - Use systems and automation. There are many low-cost solutions at your disposal to support you in building, segmenting, and nurturing your list. At a minimum, I recommend that you use a reliable email marketing tool. If you are just starting out, something like MailChimp will give you the basic functionality needed to create, segment, and communicate to your email list. Eventually, you will want to transition to a more robust CRM, customer relationship management system. At BSN, we currently use Active Campaign, and it has been great for us. To sign up or learn more about Active Campaign you can use our affiliate link http://bit.ly/bsnemails

Do – Give Value Before Asking for Something. Each person on your list is looking to solve a problem. For your audience, create ways to share your content and demonstrate your expertise. For your clients, take the time to understand the goals for their organization and offer ways to make their job easier. Never SPAM people or add people to an email list before asking permission. If someone requests to be removed from your email or mailing list, do so immediately.

Do – Be Creative. How will you cut through the clutter of all the other speakers and proposals sent to meeting planners? Do you customize each proposal, send handwritten notes, or send personalized videos? The person most remembered is the person most hired. You do not need to be like anyone else. Use your unique personality and strengths to win others over in your own special way.

Do Not – Talk badly about others. People will upset you; deals will fall through, situations will disappoint you, but you never want to develop a reputation as a person who bad mouths other people. Again, this is a long-term business. Word gets around, so if you talk poorly about your leads, clients, or anyone in your network, even if that person never finds out, you will diminish the trust you have with others.

Do Not – Break Your Commitments. Your word means a lot in the speaking business, and it travels fast when you do not honor your commitments. If you owe your clients or audience something, always provide it when you say you will or provide updates on when they can expect it. If you make a mistake, admit it, do your best to fix it and move on.

Do Not - Do it alone. The speaking business can be a lonely place. One of the reasons I created Black Speakers Network is so that I would not have to go on this journey by myself, especially when there are so many people walking the same path. Make an effort to reach out to other speakers (even your competition) and build relationships. Learn from others and share your knowledge as well.

If you need help finding your stage and building a strategy to stay consistently booked, I invite you to join Black Speakers Network today. Before you go to the next chapter, **take 30 seconds to get started now at www.BlackSpeakersNetwork.com**

Speak Up! Your Audience Awaits...

BRIAN J. OLDS

Brian J. Olds wasn't born with a natural enthusiasm for public speaking.

A burgeoning change agent in the industry, the Baltimore native inadvertently entered into the world of speaking when he delivered his first speech to the *Morgan State University* Toastmasters Club in 2006. Recalling this as one of his most defining life moments, Brian instantly connected to his passion when he found himself in front of a standing ovation at the conclusion of that speech.

Identified as a "curator of collaboration," Brian specializes in empowering rising professional speakers to create clarity, streamline systems, and cultivate the relationships needed to reach the unique audience they are called to serve. His passion for speaking, diversity and building relationships led him to create *Black Speakers Network* (BSN), a membership-based professional speaker development and empowerment association. With thousands of members around the world, BSN holds the distinction of being the most accessible and fastest growing development organization, dedicated to serving underrepresented speakers at all levels in their career.

Recognized as one of the brightest talents with a unique mix of corporate, academic and leadership, Brian's influence and prowess has warranted favorable opportunities to showcase his talent and spread awareness, beyond BSN. In 2015, he competed in the *Toastmasters International Speech Contest*, a competition with over 30,000 participants who compete for a chance to take part in the *World Championship of Public Speaking®*. Brian proudly advanced to the semi-finals, competing against the top 100 speakers around the world.

With a deep appreciation for the artistry of speaking at the helm of his career, Brian J Olds is defining success on his own terms. His impact is illustrated perfectly in industry mate Zig Ziglar's quote, "It's not where you start – it's where you finish that counts."

www.BlackSpeakersNetwork.com
www.instagram.com/BlackSpeakersNetwork
www.Facebook.com/BlackSpeakersNetwork

YOUR AUDIENCE IN THE PALM OF YOUR HAND!

UNLOCKING THE POWER OF LIVE VIDEO

ALTOVISE PELTZER

Video is the new flat screen television in a world still hooked on the big floor model television. (You know the one that was broken with the smaller television on top of it. Lol) It is interesting and new but so many Speakers still believe they either 1 Cannot afford it or 2 Cannot figure out how to use it. There are many tools that contribute to the foundation of a successfully paid speaker and video is one of the resources people often leave off the list. Ultimately, you are leaving money on the table by NOT using video as a part of your speaking business.

Let's talk numbers!

Video, especially live stream, has allowed Speakers from all over the world to increase their revenue and reach. Imagine getting on stage before thousands of your targeted listeners at one event a year. (Sounds amazing, right?) Well, video allows you to get in front of them day after day for absolutely FREE! Well, not completely free… there is the cost of internet and your monthly cell phone bill, but you get my point.

You are probably wondering why more speakers are not using this tool. I am glad you brought that point up.

"My people are destroyed for lack of knowledge…"
– Hosea 4:6

I have seen speakers leap into the realm of video with little to no understanding and no strategy. The result is often a crash and burn scenario after a few months. That being said, I want to put you on the right track by highlighting some of the video and live stream myths floating around. I will also set you up with my personal Live Stream Toolkit that my clients use to get started. The MOST important thing for you to remember is that this is one of many tools that can help you as a speaker.

MYTH

Before we jump into the money-making, list building, live stream machine, let's knock out a few myths. These strategies will produce short term and long-term results. As a Speaker, Live Streaming can be an inexpensive marketing tool or an expensive hobby. Either way, knowing what the myths are upfront will save you time, money, and energy.

Myth 1: Live Stream is fast cash!

It can be but do not start with that mindset. While live stream has given people ALL over the world the ability to make money… it is not as simple as showing up with a link. There is a strategy to this. Live Streaming is a great tool to build the "know, like, and trust" factor with potential clients and customers.

Myth 2: It is expensive to Live Stream!

Nope, wrong again! (In my Rafiki voice) Most of you have the essential tools to get started which are a phone and a live streaming app. Do not get me wrong, there are plenty of tools that can range upwards of $12,000 - $30,000 per year. Those are more for bigger brands with a larger marketing budget.

Myth 3: I need to wait for people to show up on the Live Stream before I start talking...

This is beyond annoying! When you Live Stream, the replay viewers are gold. The three minutes you spend waiting for people to show up or spend inviting people is dead air to replay viewers. They may not make it past that to hear what you are sharing on the broadcast. Imagine someone standing in front of the room for three minutes not saying anything while waiting for people to come back from the bathroom. Yup... just like that.

Myth 4: I need an excessive amount of content to go live!

Content is everywhere and as a speaker anytime you open your mouth to talk about a topic relevant to your industry you are sharing content. Do not get hung up on having the perfect outline of what you want to share. As people show up the topic may be redirected from questions and dialogue.

Myth 5: If I Live Stream an event people will not buy tickets!

This is actually the opposite of the truth. When you live stream an event you are adding another revenue stream for your event. People can now watch from all over the world which gives you a broader audience. Let's do the math. If you add a $29 live stream ticket to your event and 100 people purchase tickets, you just added 100 people to your audience and $2,900 to your revenue. Looks like a win/win to me.

Now that we have covered some of the many myths that have been circulating the internet streets, let's get to the tips you need to get started. The mastery of something requires dedication and consistency. Speakers such as Dr. Maya Angelou or Dr. Les Brown did not get to their level of expertise without them. As a speaker, you are saying that you are dedicated to your topic and that you will consistently deliver. It does not mean that you are perfect or that you know everything there is to know.

MASTERY

I have heard every excuse possible for why speakers are not using video.

- Need a new wardrobe
- Waiting until they lose a few pounds
- Introvert or shy
- Do not have the time

As an introvert, I definitely understand your fears and I am here to give you a boost to your confidence. First, let me say that video gives you access. Now you may be asking yourself... access to what? You have access to Malcolm Gladwell's 10,000-hour rule or the 80+ speaking events that Dr. Maya Angelou would do in a year. In the palm of your hand, you have access to the experience you need to elevate your speaking business.

What does access do? You are now able to share and get feedback on speech topics and keynote addresses with the push of a button. Your audience is waiting to see what you are working on. As a live streamer, I have to say that building a community is much easy through video. People want to follow your story and be inspired by your wins. They also want to see the stumbles at times because it allows them to see that their own dreams can become reality. Ultimately, you become the Empire show that everyone tunes in to watch regularly.

When you show up consistently you are able to offer books, classes, memberships, and event tickets to your viewers. You can build your email list by offering a freemium.

A freemium can be a tip sheet, an e-book, or even a challenge that engages them through an automated email sequence. (5 - 7-day challenges rank best because people do not lose interest) This can also be called a lead magnet which leads them to one of your paid products or services. We are talking dollars and cents, right? Getting them off social media and onto your email list, into a class or in a seat at your next event just got a little easier.

Are you ready to get to a mastery level of speaking on your topic? Great! I have a challenge to get you started. Go live for five days and talk to your audience. You have to go live at the same time each day and do not worry about how long you are live. Do not get nervous on me now. You can try going live in the World Voice League free Facebook Community => bit.ly/groupvoice to get some support and feedback. (I also would love to hear how you are mastering the live stream world and the Live Stream Toolkit is there) Just add #worldvoiceleague to your title along with #speakup so I can come to support you.

Be Heard 5 Day Challenge

Day 1 ~ Introduction

Day 2 ~ 3 tips in your area of expertise

Day 3 ~ What does your typical day look like?

Day 4 ~ Reminisce about your first speaking event

Day 5 ~ Freemium offer

I love giving bonuses. So, the bonus is that this challenge can be done on any social media platform and you do not have to use it with just live streaming. You can record the video on your phone and upload it to any (or all) of your social media pages. Watch your engagement begin to go up as you start empowering the world. They are waiting for you!

ALTOVISE PELTZER

 Altovise Pelzer is a Best-Selling Author, Professional Speaker, Live Streamer, Life Coach, and founder of the World Voice League. She also hosts the #SpeakEasy Podcast, your #1 Podcast for unscripted and unbiased perspectives on becoming and staying a successfully paid Author or Speaker. At her core, she is mom of four, will break out into impromptu dance parties, take a beach trip, or read a book.

Homelessness and molestation greatly affected Altovise. She hit a turning point in her life after decades of being silent about her molestation story even after finding out both her girls were molested. This was the catalyst for her decision to motivate women to "Leverage Their Life's Circumstances" by learning to love their voice. She takes women from abuse to applause by equipping them to Define, Accept and Use their Voice as a Speaker, Author or Entrepreneur.

bit.ly/wvlmember
www.instagram.com/worldvoiceleague
www.facebook.com/worldvoiceleague
www.linkedin.com/in/worldvoiceleague

YOU CANNOT BE BOOKED IF YOU CANNOT BE FOUND!

HOW TO INCREASE YOUR VISIBILITY

PAM PERRY

I taught my PR mentoring group on the "Top Ten Things That Can Ruin Your Brand Online" because branding is all about trust. Trust equals business.

Think about the last time you hired a contractor, either for your business or to do something around your home. Did you look for the lowest price, or did you look for someone with experience? Did you check the contractor's references, or just take his word at face value?

You likely have heard the old adage, "you get what you pay for," and usually, when you hire someone simply based on the lowest price, you will get someone who is not as experienced as the higher-priced contractor. Lack of experience can lead to mistakes, and sometimes they are costly. And let's face it, not everyone is as honest as you are, so if you are not checking references, you might get scammed.

What is the lesson here?

Successful businesses stay afloat when they gain years of experience and build their credibility with their audience. These business owners learn from their own mistakes, adjust the way they do business when something does not work and are willing to share their knowledge with their clients prior to being hired.

Fans will flock to businesses with a good track record and good customer reviews. It stands to reason that an influx of customers means hiring more team members and making more sales, thereby growing your business.

Now let's put YOU into this equation. You should always charge what you are worth because if you undercut your competition, that will bring in the tire kickers who are not serious customers and may still ask you for a discount. This is not the audience base that will allow your business to grow.

You should also showcase your expertise online and offline. Never be afraid to market yourself because you cannot control the search engine rankings and you do not want to depend on 'hope' marketing. That is a very passive way to run your business; HOPING that people will find you. Be visible online and offline, be vocal, tell people what you do, share your experiences, and offer advice. THIS will build your credibility and you will gain more visibility, thereby gaining new followers and potential new clients.

No matter what stage of business you are in today, whether you just opened your doors or have had a string of clients for years, today is the day to concentrate on building your credibility and sharing your expertise with the world.

This is no time to be a wallflower, especially if you have big dreams of growing your team, hitting a certain income milestone, selling a certain number of products, or booking a guest appearance on The Today Show. Be proud of your success and plan on sharing it with your audience.

Do not be the world's best-kept secret. Get out there! PR can help and so can partnering.

Ask nearly anyone who runs an online business what their biggest struggle is and chances are they will say, "more traffic."

You need traffic to build an email list. You need traffic to make sales. You need traffic to fill your coaching programs and get speaking gigs. So, the big question is, where do you get all that traffic?

You could buy ads, but if you are not careful, you might fill your list with less-than-ideal audience members and that will do nothing for your sales. You could focus your time and energy on search engine optimization but unless you have years to build your business (and who does?) then SEO should not be your top choice.

Good thing you have other options like these:

Be a Guest

Everyone needs content. It is the one thing that remains consistent among all content creators - there is never enough. That is where you can help. By guest posting on other coaches' blogs, you can "borrow" some of their traffic.

You cannot simply regurgitate old content and send it out in a dozen directions though. To get the best results, you will want to:

- Create custom content designed with your host's unique audience in mind.

- Provide stellar value with actionable ideas and strategies not found everywhere else.

- Inject your personality so those new to you will instantly connect with you.

- Offer a compelling reason to click through to your website or blog for more information.

Partner Up

No list? Here's a quick way to "borrow" someone else's list to kickstart your own: Schedule a free event with a partner.

Here's how it works: You (as the one with the small list) create a compelling, free training which leads naturally to a low-cost, no-brainer product. Install an affiliate tracking system such as Eventbrite, Infusionsoft or 1Shopping Cart.

Offer your best affiliates a higher percentage of profits in exchange for co-hosting your webinar and bringing their traffic along for the ride.

This is a win/win for both of you, as you gain the traffic while your affiliate gets a bigger payday. Just be sure you have a good funnel in place so that your new list members can benefit from all that you have to offer.

Get Interviewed

Want to really show off your expert status and bring traffic back to your site, too? The easiest way is to get on the interview circuit. Try podcasts or local talk radio shows. Just like authors with new books and actors with new movies, coaches and service providers can get in front of new audiences simply by answering questions about what they know.

You are probably not going to appear on the Today Show or Oprah (although that is possible), but there are still plenty of opportunities out there for coaches and consultants in every niche.

Look for interview and speaking opportunities on:
- Podcasts
- Other blogs
- YouTube
- Facebook Live
- Local events

Speak Up!

- Industry conferences
- Telesummits

Start by reaching out to your colleagues and to podcast and blog hosts you most admire. Get the word out with your friends and your list that you are looking for opportunities.

Even if you do not yet have a list of your own, it is easy (and fun) to kickstart your audience growth simply by making yourself available for these and other opportunities.

Each guest post, podcast interview, and webinar is another chance to get in front of a whole new market, so take advantage of it!

PAM PERRY

 Pam Perry is an award-winning communications professional. She teaches and mentors authors, speakers, and entrepreneurs on how to build a platform and attract major media and publishers. She is also the publisher of Speakers Magazine and founder of the National Association of Black Podcasters.

After working with Pam, her clients have been featured on CNN, TBN, The Word Network, Radio One, Oprah Magazine, Tom Joyner Morning Show, Essence, Ebony, Black Enterprise, PBS – and many other major media outlets. Her clients have been offered major publishing contracts and have created successful full-time careers as "authorpreneurs" earning six-figures.

She has been called by Publishers Weekly a "PR Guru" and featured in many major publications (including several covers), and on more than 100 radio and TV programs. She also has a 20-year career expertise in marketing, public relations, and journalism in Detroit; including work with The Detroit Free Press, WNIC, The Edge with Jeffrey Miller, Radio One, Michigan Chronicle, WNIC and TheHUB Detroit magazine.

Pam has worked with many nonprofit organizations, like the Charles H. Wright Museum of African American History and the Detroit Area Agency on Aging, developing their social media presence, online brand, and digital marketing programs. She is also author of Synergy Energy: How to Use the Power of Partnerships to Market Your Book, Grow Your Business and Brand Your Ministry and 115 PR Tips on How to Brand Your Ministry (both available on Amazon.com).

Known as the master of connecting the right people, for the right project, at the right time – Pam Perry PR works hard to help her clients' brand (and get paid) like a superstar.

www.pamperrypr.com
www.linkedin.com/in/pamperryprcoach
www.instagram.com/pam_perry
www.twitter.com/thespeakersmag

PLAN BEFORE YOU POST!
BUILDING A SOCIAL MEDIA STRATEGY FOR YOUR SPEAKING BUSINESS
KEISHA REYNOLDS

Why Social?

In the current state of online marketing, I believe that we can effectively answer the question of *"why does my business need to be on social media?"* If you are still stuck there, this chapter is not for you, you have to do some deeper soul searching to find that answer. This chapter is for you if you have an online presence but struggle with what to post, how to engage your audience and how to effectively position yourself as an expert on your subject matter.

The very nature of social media is the premise of being social. Many times, businesses miss this underlying truth in the pursuit of understanding their individual purpose for using social media as a marketing tool. Not only is social media a new communications outlet, but it has also changed the essence of how we communicate across every medium that precedes it. With one post, you can create a conversation or invoke a thought that transcends geographical locations, age, race, and gender. That is how powerful social media is in the life of any business.

Being a speaker is no different. You can use a speech that you deliver on stage to hundreds of people as your value-based idea for using social media. This simply means, identifying a simple concept that sits at the heart of your speaking business which will drive the value that you deliver to your followers each day. To determine this, you have to look at being a speaker as a brand to determine your brand positioning so that when online users think of a particular subject, they deem you as a thought-leader in the social space on that matter. This then creates what we call a tribe of followers that seek you for knowledge and will advocate for you online without you having to ask them.

Find Your Tribe

This now leads me to the idea of finding your tribe online. Social media is much like real life whereas you need people to support your dreams and ideas. Much like you acquire a circle of friends, creating your tribe is built on trust, consistency, and value. Each of these elements brings your followers to consider you their "go to" person within your speaking niche. You create this by providing content and messaging that resonates with their lives. One key to developing your tribe is to be authentic. People connect with people. Tapping into what makes you unique will allow you to stand out in a saturated market. Another key to doing this is to value your audience's attention. They are people and much like you, your followers do not want to have their time wasted. This means, to only create content when you truly have something relevant to say instead of the first things that come to your mind. Strategically planning your posts will always lead you in the right direction.

The Social Plan for Speakers

A strategy is the key to your online success as a speaker. The main proponent of your strategy is going to be based on content and what you ultimately want a singular piece of content to do for your speaking business. If you struggle to develop content, it is because you do not view yourself as a brand. A brand consistently creates content around what they do and who they serve. To do this as a speaker, you will need the three focus areas I have outlined below.

1. **Social Proof:** There is a level of psychology when it comes to online marketing. Behaviors influence when your audience decides to click, share, favorite, or purchase from your social platform. Understanding human interaction helps you to discern your audience and why they react to one form of content over another. Essentially, creating content that reinforces your expertise as a speaker will allow you to win in the eyes of your audience. You can do this through four basic fundamentals: Testimonials, Collaboration, Milestones, and Press.

   o Get participants from your speaking engagements to provide video-based testimonials of experiencing your presentation. Notice that I mentioned video instead of a written testimonial. This is because in the digital age people want content that they can view quickly verse read. Not only that, but video is king when it comes to content creation. Video helps to attract, retain, and convert your viewers. It receives a higher percentage of organic reach than photos and many marketers will tell you that it directly impacts your return on investment. In 2018, we witnessed how our social platforms placed an extreme focus on video (Instagram Stories, IGTV, Facebook Stories, YouTube Stories). If you are not creating video-based testimonials, you are missing a huge part of your audience. This also allows your viewers to see, in real-time, your impact and influence on those that you come to hear you speak.

○ Collaboration is the key to life. If you want to grow in business, partnering with others is one way to do it. Collaborating with macro and micro influencers in your niche will help to increase your social reach. You can do this through scheduled Instagram Lives, Instagram Takeovers or joint webinars. This helps to further solidify your expertise among your audience; especially, if they follow or know of the person you collaborate with online.

○ Milestones are perfect because people love celebrations. Choose which milestones you will highlight such as reaching a new peak with your number of followers, a book launch, major speaking engagements, featured articles, or a new certification in your niche.

○ If your work has allowed you to be featured in the press, that is huge social proof! Share any television segments, news articles, radio clips, blog posts or podcasts where you have been featured. This simply strengthens your relationship with your followers to view you as an expert.

2. **Humanize Your Online Self:** I mentioned this earlier in the chapter whereas people connect with people. Your followers want you to be authentic, genuine, and relatable. You have to have a balance between your personality and professional life. Bring your followers into the preparation of your next speaking engagement, give a behind-the-scenes look before you step onto the stage, capture real-time photos and videos of your live audience, and share it with your followers, or ask your followers what are some areas that they need help with as it relates to your speaking niche. A powerful aspect of humanizing your online self is storytelling. Tell your followers a story. Did you learn something new in your research? Did you learn something new from a member of the audience that witnessed your speech that you can relate to? Why did you decide to focus on your speaking topics? What highlights can you share?

3. **Create Content that Sales:** This one will be easier to produce. It will help you to define what you should post and how to create brand awareness for increased engagement online. Once you find your tribe, talk to them about your ideas and allow them to share their thoughts and questions with you. This can help you develop new focus areas for your postings. You can also utilization user-generated content from your speaking engagement. If you took a photo with someone or they posted a video clip of you speaking, repurpose that content. The next idea that I want to share with you is to use the main points of your subject matter to develop content for your social media platforms. Break down the essence of your speech into smaller, more digestible

pieces of content for your online messaging and posts. Lastly, with each post that you create, you should have a call-to-action. What do you want your followers to do as a result of viewing a particular piece of content?

Thinking of each of these will allow you to effectively strategize and create content that resonates and enhances your online presence.

What is Next?

Continue to educate yourself on social media trends related to business and personal brands. Attending workshops, seminars, and webinars on this topic as well as being a part of coaching programs, will increase your understanding and enhance your skills. The landscape of social media is ever-changing which means that you have to be a continued learner in order to have a competitive advantage within your industry.

As you exit this chapter, I want to encourage you to do two things before you begin implementing any new strategies in your social presence. The first is to conduct a social media audit. In order to know what is working and what is not working, you have to assess your online activities. A part of your audit is also your strategy - this means that you need to think of your goals as you assess your current works. Notice what is enhancing your message and what is filler content that lacks purpose. You will also need to identify any social media accounts that are stagnant or no longer in use, please control, alt, delete those accounts. Focus in on the social platforms where your audience is most engaged or most active (this will require research). Highlight the type of content that appeals to your audience based on likes, comments, and shares. Your social media audit will reveal to you the relevancy of your content, consistency in your social channels, and your true return on investment.

The final piece and I cannot stress this enough, is to check the quality of your content. The truth is you are a brand, so you have to show up in the social media space as one. Your imagery, videos, text-based posts should all be high-quality content. Not only does it help in establishing your credibility online, content branding is also a major part of your content marketing strategy. Each post that you create should have a purpose and it should resonate with your followers. I want to encourage you to not depend on recycling content that you see within the internet world. Your content must show your brand's personality and provide your audience with the information they need and want. If your goal is to truly become the expert for your followers online, then your content should have a level of excellence connected to it because it is a visual representation of your work and worth as a speaker.

KEISHA REYNOLDS

Keisha Kay Reynolds is best defined as kinetic. She puts things in motion and believes in the power of community. Keisha is the CEO of K&R Communications, a branding and digital marketing agency for small businesses, churches, and nonprofits throughout the East Coast. Keisha has published work on social media for higher education, and she speaks around the country on its use for churches. Not only that, but she is also a professor at Hampton University in the Scripps Howard School of Journalism and Communications where she leads the web development curriculum and teaches public relations. Keisha holds a Master of Arts in Media and Communications from Norfolk State University and a Bachelor of Science in Journalism and Technical Communication from Ferris State University. In addition, she is the beauty behind the brand of EmpoweringHER, a women's empowerment organization for business and self-care. Most recently, Keisha was inducted into the 2018 class of M-Lifestyle Magazine's Top 30 Under 40 receiving this honor with several Millennial-based entrepreneurs across the world (U.S., U.K., and Africa).

www.KNRagency.com
@_KeishaKay
@KRCommunications

SPREAD YOUR VOICE TO THE WORLD!

UNLOCKING THE POWER OF PODCASTING

KANIKA TOLVER

In the past five years, podcasting has become popular amongst influencers, authors, and speakers. It is a great way to build your brand and an even better way for listeners to see you speak on video or via audio. The best way to begin spreading your voice is to become a featured guest on podcast shows. As a speaker, you will interact with the podcast host, responding to questions and simply having an authentic conversation about your personal brand and subject matter expertise.

The great thing about podcasting is that you can constantly market these podcast episodes to your viewers, your followers, and the world using social media and email marketing. You never know who may be listening to your awesome podcast interviews that may want to contact you for a paid speaking engagement. In 2018, I created my own podcast tour, which helped me land several paid speaking gigs at the Blacks in Technology (BIT) conference and several colleges. I speak mainly on career development, women in technology, and entrepreneurship, so I have developed a network of partnerships with podcast show hosts that focus on those topics.

You must be strategic throughout the process of creating a speaking presence through podcasting, determining which type of podcast shows you want to spread your voice on. I have created a 4-step process that has helped me land over 20 podcast interviews in less than one year. This process will help you find the right podcast for your message, as well as learn how to speak well in your interviews and how to market them to the world.

Find the Right Podcast Shows

First, you need to create a spreadsheet of all the podcast show names, focus areas, and contact information. Research podcast shows by searching for keywords or subjects that align with your brand's messaging as a speaker. The best way to find podcast shows is by using the hashtags #podcast #podcastshow #podcasting on Twitter and Instagram. You can also search for podcast shows using Google. For example: "technology podcast shows." Add all of this podcast information to your spreadsheet. Also, make sure you find an email address for the podcast show and/or host so you can pitch yourself to the show.

Pitch Yourself to Podcast Shows

The best way to land an interview is by pitching yourself to podcast shows that align with your brand and message. First, you want to develop an email template that introduces yourself and brand to the podcast show host. Next, you need to listen to one episode to determine if you would be a good fit for the show. Then, email the podcast show team, attaching your speaker one sheet, speaker biography, website information, and social media information. You want the podcast show host to have enough information about your brand and speaking topics to easily determine if you are a good fit for their show.

Be Authentic and Enthusiastic

Now that you are booked for the podcast show, you need to bring your A-game. If the recording will include video, you have a better opportunity to pretend like you are on the stage. You can unlock your voice on the podcast by displaying energy and authenticity. If the podcast recording is audio-only, then you need to speak clearly, always smile as you speak and make the show sound like a real conversation rather than just question and answer. You want people to identify your speaking style on your podcast interviews; reuse your speaking materials in your interview responses. Also, share real-life stories and experiences on the podcast show, because listeners love transparent and down to earth guests.

Market Your Podcast Interview

The key to spreading your voice is using online marketing. Once your podcast interview has been edited and produced by the podcast host, you can start marketing it on your personal website, social media, and via email marketing. Remember to use content related hashtags for your social media posts. Also, embed the podcast show recording within your website and add the URL link in your email newsletter. Another great way to spread your voice is by having your friends and family members share your podcast interviews on their social media accounts. You should market the podcast interviews every week for about 4-8 weeks to ensure all of your followers get a chance to see to listen to your interview.

As you spread your voice to the world make sure you have fun doing it. It is important to unlock your voice by enjoying your interview recordings and being proud of the content you deliver through the power of the internet. Also, create a fun marketing strategy as you spread your voice to the world. Remember, the world is waiting to hear the real you and the speaker inside of you.

KANIKA TOLVER

Kanika Tolver is no ordinary "social-preneur." This highly decorated government employee turned rebel entrepreneur and Certified Professional Coach is a serial innovator who's fueled by an extraordinary commitment to social change and to helping others create their own "epic lives." As an in-demand coach, consultant, speaker and thought leader who's often tapped as an expert source for the media, Tolver helps individuals establish themselves at the "architect of their own life" to realize career, business, life, and spiritual success—all in a way that promotes restoration, balance and nurturing one's authentic self. Her services include career coaching and technology coaching. A self-professed "tech geek" and career technologist enamored by the latest and greatest gadgetry, Tolver is also an advocate who also promotes "people of color" getting more involved in science and technology. Tolver is a highly regarded source often tapped by the press, having been featured on CNN, CBS Radio, Yahoo, Glassdoor, Entrepreneur, the Washington Post and in a litany of radio interviews. Kanika Tolver, who graduated from Bowie State University in Maryland, currently hails from Washington, DC where she has resided most of her life.

www.kanikatolver.com
www.twitter.comKanikaTolver
www.instagram.KanikaTolver
www.linkedin.com/in/kanikatolver

CTRL+ALT+DEL

HOW YOUR SPEAKER WEBSITE MAY BE TURNING OFF YOUR CLIENTS

DANIELLE TUCKER

TRAVEL. SPEAK. RINSE. REPEAT.

As a professional speaker, attending conferences, meetings, and in-person events is a regular part of your lifestyle. And with all of the hustle and excitement that comes with traveling and meeting new people, it is also important that you have a trusty 24/7 sidekick that can keep up with your busy schedule. This is not any ordinary "sidekick." Think of this…

A sidekick that can give you confidence that if you forget sharing that one super important piece of information with your new contact at an event - You do not have to worry! It has got you covered.

A sidekick that can instantly boost your credibility, convert more sales, and nurture new people so that they know, like, and trust you as a leading expert in your industry.

A sidekick that can give you peace of mind, that whenever you pass out a business card to new contacts, each person will have everything they need to begin working with you, all in the palm of their hands.

This sidekick may sound like a superhuman assistant, but the biggest difference is that it does not sleep, and it can work for you even when you are getting a good night's rest to prepare for your next engagement.

This sidekick is none other than your professional speaker website! When designed correctly, your speaker website has the potential to move mountains for you. But when done incorrectly, it could seriously be turning off your clients and repelling some really important business.

But do not worry! I have got your back! In this chapter, I am going to share with you some of the most common mistakes that speakers make that repel clients from their websites, along with the best solutions to make sure these mistakes do not happen to you.

1. No Clear Goal to Drive Your Viewer's Clicks

What is the purpose of a speaker website anyway? When launching a new speaker website, many speakers aim to have a website that looks "pretty." Yes, first impressions are important, and your online home should look presentable, but you could still be repelling clients by ignoring a very important step.

The secret behind a successful speaker website that converts is that you need to have a clear end goal that will lead your viewers to take a specific action.

Not having a clear end goal is a common mistake that most speakers make. In order to make sure that you do not make the same mistake, let's start by asking these 3 important questions.

1. What is the purpose behind your new speaker website?

2. What end goal do you hope to accomplish with your speaker website?

3. What main action do you want your viewers to take, after they enter your website?

By answering these questions, you are now able to create a clear plan of action for where you want your viewers to go. Although it might seem simple, this is one of the biggest steps that can differentiate a successful speaker website from a website that flops. Always remember to set a clear end goal!

2. Not Having a Speaker Video Could Be Hindering Your Conversions By 144%!

Another crucial mistake that speakers make is not having a speaker video reel on your website. Your speaker video is a non-negotiable on your site, especially since using video has the potential to increase your site conversions by 144%. Your speaker video will help you to deliver a very specific message that cannot be fully conveyed with written words or pictures alone. A few of these benefits include:

1. Showcasing your unique speaking style - When event organizers, booking agents, and potential clients come to visit your speaker website, they are curious to see your speaking style. Video is a great tool to help you get your message out there, in order to teach and inform the people who are looking to learn from you the most.

2. Showcase your personality - People buy from people that they know, like, and trust. In order to build this, know, like, and trust factor within your speaker business, you also must create opportunity for people to feel like they have connected with you. Your speaker video is a great tool to help you showcase your personality.

3. Give a preview of your experience - When you are speaking, you are in your element. You feel confident and excited because you know that you are living your passion and your message is changing the lives of those who are engaging with you. This very passion is the same element that your audience wants to see when watching your videos. Not only does it get them excited about working with you, but it also boosts your credibility as an expert in your field.

Overall, video is a true game changer when it comes to showcasing your expertise as a speaker. If you want to directly increase the rate by which you receive conversions and book more speaking engagements, adding video to your site is a great place to start.

3. What You Do Not Know CAN Hurt You!

The last mistake that speakers often make is underestimating/not knowing the power of a strategic and well-crafted speaker website. An effective speaker website has the potential to open a flood of opportunities for you. Here are some of the proven benefits...

- easily raise and justify your speaking fees

- build brand awareness

- boost your speaking credibility

- grow your network through email list building

- sell your services, books, and digital products online

- showcase your speaking style and expertise through video

- standout and impress booking agents and event organizers

- reach more people in your local & international audiences

- be recognized as an expert in your field

And the list goes on!

If you are looking to launch your new speaker website or refresh a current site, here are some next best steps to help you move in the right direction.

1. Find a style you love. - We are often drawn to styles that match our own unique creativity. To make sure that your new site is creatively inspired and built to match your unique taste, it is a good idea to create a list of inspirational websites. Start by searching sites of your favorite speakers/mentors or using a tool like Pinterest.com to create an inspiration board. After you have created your list, you can deliver this to a designer as a source of inspiration so they can understand your style.

2. Search for an experienced designer that understands the speaking industry. - Before you invest in your new speaker website, make sure that you ALWAYS ask your potential designer these very important questions. "Have you ever built a website for a speaker before?" "How many years have you been designing websites?" "Do you have a portfolio I can review?" "Do you have references/testimonials?" "What is the design timeline?" "What is the cost of working together?" By asking these questions you will be one step closer to making the best decision for your speaker website.

3. Set a date and commit to launching your new site. - Have you ever heard the phrase… "If it is not on the calendar, it is not real."? The same is true for your speaker website. A great way to ensure you get the most impact from your speaker website is to pencil in a start date that will compliment your schedule and upcoming events. For example, do you have a big international engagement coming up? Are you planning to launch your first event? With all of the new visibility, your audience will be searching for a place to engage with you online.

To avoid any delays with potential business, make sure that you plan the launch of your site well in advance of your special engagements. This will save you lots of time, money, and stress in the long run.

As a professional speaker, booking new engagements, nurturing your audience, closing more sales, and growing your online visibility does not have to be tricky business. It can be easy, especially with the help of your trusty 24/7 sidekick: your speaker website. So, the next time you strike up a conversation at an event, or decide to hand out a business card, do not stress. Remember that your speaker website has got your back, and it can help to make all the difference!

DANIELLE TUCKER

Danielle Tucker is the Founder and Creative Director of Professional Speaker Websites, a web design agency built to support professional speakers, authors, and coaches that speak. For over 4 years, she's helped professional speakers to stand out online by using her signature Speaker Website Framework, a framework designed to help speakers convert more clients, be recognized as the leading experts in their niche, and book more speaking engagements. With a proven track record of success, Danielle's mission is to help more speakers to stand out online so they can book more speaking engagements, and more powerfully impact the people that they're called to serve.

www.ProfessionalSpeakerWebsites.com
www.facebook.com/ProfessionalSpeakerWebsites
www.instagram.com/ProfessionalSpeakerWebsites

IS YOUR NETWORK INCREASING YOUR NET WORTH?

HOW TO LEVERAGE LINKEDIN AS A SPEAKER

ROBERT YOUNGBLOOD

LinkedIn is the most powerful, yet underrated and underutilized social networking platform on the planet. What started out as a website for job seekers and recruiters, morphed into a tremendous resource for business owners, entrepreneurs, sales professionals, and speakers. Are you using LinkedIn just to promote yourself as a speaker or are you positioning yourself as a problem solver?

The difference maker

If you are not using LinkedIn, you are making a huge mistake and missing out on the opportunity to grow your network and net worth as a Speaker.

During the Spring of 2017, I landed a major speaking opportunity with Old Dominion University. My main point of contact found me on LinkedIn.

During our initial conversation, my client stated that he was impressed by the various speaking experiences I showcased on my LinkedIn profile. He wanted to hire someone to train his student-athletes to network and leverage LinkedIn to establish opportunities after college. He had a choice of speakers to choose from but selected me because my LinkedIn profile gave him what he needed in order to get his team to sign my contract.

It was my optimized LinkedIn profile that made the difference between me and my competitors.

Optimize your LinkedIn profile - The keys to growing your network and net worth

As a Speaker, keep the following principles in mind if you want to leverage LinkedIn to grow your network and net worth.

- Your LinkedIn profile is a living resource. It grows as you grow.

  I have learned that the more you grow as an individual, the stronger your personal story becomes. As you grow, you will be able to relate to more people. Leverage LinkedIn to tell your story. Promote your successes and your lessons learned. Doing so will make you relatable to your followers.

- Share content that addresses the problems you solve and the value you offer.

  The most important question that your LinkedIn profile should answer is "What problem do you solve"? The key to growing your network and net worth on LinkedIn is to promote your value as a problem solver.

- Your face is your logo, use a professional headshot to capture the authenticity of your personality.

  Hire a professional photographer to capture your true essence. Never use a logo for your headshot. People do business with people and not brands. Make sure you have an appealing smile with a solid color background.

- Remember, a picture is worth a thousand words. Etch your brand in the mind of your potential client by using a background photo that promotes what you do.

  LinkedIn gives your real estate on your profile in the form of a background photo. Use the space at the top of your profile to share a collage or one picture that leaves a positive impression upon all who land on your page.

- Craft a headline that promotes your value

  Instead of highlighting your title and company name in your headline, use a value statement that promotes who you are, who you help and how you help

- The summary section should be used to set you apart from other speakers

  Many people use the Summary section to share their bio. Instead, use this section to qualify your potential client. Expound upon your headline but answering the 5 most important questions: Who are you; What do you do; Why do you do what you do; Who do you help and How do you help.

- The experience section should highlight the impact you brought to every engagement

Do not use LinkedIn as a resume where you promote the task you performed in your various positions. Instead, provide an overview of each organization and highlight the impact and value you brought to each organization

- Testimonials are the key to credibility

Testimonials will seal the deal within the mind of your potential client. When someone writes a testimonial for you, it says they are willing to put their reputation on the line for you. Ask for testimonials after every engagement and have your clients post them on LinkedIn for you.

The importance of visibility & credibility

A wise man once told me, "If no one knows you exist, how can they pay you?" This question speaks to the importance of visibility. At the same time, your credibility as a speaker will determine if you will even get a shot to showcase your talent.

While sites like Facebook, Instagram and Twitter are popular for social interactions. LinkedIn's value stems from the culture of the platform, where the focus is on business and building a solid professional network.

Your value as a Speaker and your ability to increase your net worth is contingent upon your capacity to increase your visibility and credibility. Visibility is the degree to which something has attracted general attention. Credibility is the quality of being trusted and believed in.

In general, networking is about building trust and mutual benefit. It is not about adding followers as much as it is about establishing genuine relationships. LinkedIn will enable you to connect with decision-makers who have similar professional interests and a desire to solve a specific problem. Position yourself as a problem solver on LinkedIn and you will never have to chase down a new client. Your network and your net worth will grow simultaneously.

ROBERT YOUNGBLOOD

Robert T. "YB" Youngblood is the Founder and Chief Connecting Officer of YBConnects, LLC, a Richmond, VA based Strategic Relationship & Referral Marketing Firm. As a Master Connector, Coach & Consultant, "YB" empowers Entrepreneurs, Professional Speakers, Sales Professionals and Students to increase Brand Awareness, Referrals and Revenue.

In many circles, "YB" is known as the "LinkedIn Locksmith" for his ability to help his clients unlock the Power of LinkedIn to increase their Visibility, Credibility and Profitability. Within the past few years, he has helped hundreds of Professionals to "Level Up on LinkedIn;" to include a Super Bowl Champion turned Entrepreneur; the number one Motivational Speaker in the World; along with Top Coaches & Consultants.

For over 15 years, 'YB' has focused his energy on building long-term relationships. His positive attitude enhances his ability to encourage people to overcome life challenges. His mission is to eradicate the poverty mindset that prevents people from becoming successful, wealthy, and rich by promoting the acquisition of Social Capital.

YB holds a bachelor's degree in Business Administration from Virginia Union University. He was born and raised in

Speak Up!

the South Bronx, NY, and now resides in Richmond, VA with his wife and two daughters. In his time off, he loves to sing, travel to warm places with palm trees and watch inspirational videos of Dr. Eric Thomas & Dr. Myles Munroe.

www.YBConnects.com
www.linkedin.com/in/ybconnects
www.instagram.com/yourlinkedinlocksmith

Monetize!

*This section will provide tips to generate multiple
streams of revenue for your speaking business*

CASH IN ON COURSES!

UNLOCKING THE POWER OF ONLINE COURSES

DUPÉ ALERU

In the world we live in today, time is our most valuable commodity. And because we value our time more than anything — outside of our health, family, and basic necessities to survive — we will do almost anything to conserve our precious time.

For example, think about when someone calls you. Twenty-five years ago — when cell phones were not mainstream — you would rush to your landline to answer the phone. Nowadays if someone calls you, you almost feel annoyed that they are calling you on their time and not your own. Thankfully for the invention of text messaging, it is a much more convenient way to communicate with people on your own time.

If you take a look at some of the world's largest brands — Uber, Netflix, and Amazon — what do they have in common? If your response is somewhere along the lines of, "They all understand their consumers' value of time," then you are correct.

Over the years as my schedule became busier, I had less time to watch television in the evenings. I was spending over $100 per month on cable, yet not watching anything at all. I finally decided to take the plunge in 2017 to disconnect my cable — something that I have had continuously since I was a child. The first few months were great! I gained back so much time that I used it to pour into my career, but because I am such a homebody, I began to get restless. I needed a great movie here and there to take a break from my workload, Netflix and Hulu eventually came to the rescue. Both media services provided me with the most convenient way to catch up on shows during my spare time. I also began to shop online, Amazon becoming my favorite e-commerce site due to its fast delivery and many perks. And let's face it, Uber is simple, affordable, and convenient, so I included that in my repertoire of easy living.

Online learning is no different — offering convenience and flexibility. It has been on the rise in recent years and according to Forbes (article written by TJ McCue), The Global Newswire predicts that the global e-learning market will reach $325 billion by 2025. With that being said, I think it is safe to say that e-learning is the future of education.

Why online courses? According to an article written by Len Markidan, online courses made $46 billion dollars in 2017. That is a BILLION with a B! If you were not paying attention a few moments ago, I am pretty sure you are wide awake now; and you are probably asking yourself, "How can I turn my information into a money-making course?" You can begin by packaging your knowledge so that it provides informative and sustainable solutions for your target audience.

But before I share the three strategies that will help you cash in on your premium course, I want you to rest assured that online courses are here to stay. Therefore, rather than rushing to get any course out to the market, I suggest that you take your time assessing your market demands so that you can get the right course out, thus maximizing your earning potential.

Strategy #1: Define Your Target Audience

Now that you have seen the numbers, you understand that there is massive market potential for just about anyone who is an expert in a particular field or marketplace. The question that you must first ask yourself is, "What do I know, that other people need to know and are willing to pay a premium price to learn it?" It is crucial that you understand who your target audience is prior to getting started with your course.

One of the mistakes that I often come across when helping people create their course curriculum, is that they try to cast too wide a net and end up empty-handed. In other words, trying to solve a problem for everyone most likely will run you into the possibility of not appealing to anyone. A more effective way to creating your course is to come up with a niche topic that ties into your target audiences pain point, and then creating your course goals to be the solution to the problem.

Once you have pinpointed your target audiences pain point, you are ready to construct a feasible plan of action that will note the courses learning objectives and outcomes.

Strategy #2: Provide a Solution to the Problem

Every course must have its learning objectives and learning outcomes. The learning objective is the general intended purposes and desired learning outcomes for the course, and the framework for assessing the effectiveness of the course. Whereas the learning outcomes describe the essential learning that the learners have achieved and can reliably demonstrate at the end of the course.

It is imperative that you, the course creator, are clear on the goals and objectives for your course. If it is unclear to you, then most likely it will be unclear to your learner. The easiest way to come up with learning objectives is to choose 3-5 objectives, your learner must know, and 3-5 outcomes, what your learner must do in order to learn it. Think of it like this, the learning objective is the knowledge, skills, and attitude that needs to be learned. And the learning outcomes are the activities that your learners will partake in so that they may meet the learning objectives.

Strategy #3: Evaluate the Outcome

The point of having an online course is to simplify a skill set that allows one to cut through information to find what is important, in other words, a shortcut to an outcome. The essential question that you must keep in mind at all times is, "How will my learners be different after taking my course?"

This question allows you to brainstorm backward so that you can be sure to hit your course benefits and goals. When you clearly understand the journey that your learner will partake in, then you can effectively provide the transformation needed to meet the learning outcome. Always choose the most impactful transformation by providing a lot of value, but by also eliminating unnecessary fluff.

Creating an online course is a process and a process that should be well thought out. If you are able to define your target audience, provide a solution to a problem, and evaluate the outcome of the learner's experience, then you are well on your way to begin creating the written lesson plans for your course.

Cheers to cashing in on your course and unlocking your inner genius!

Dupé Aleru

Dupé Aleru is a four-time published author, international award-winning speaker, and curriculum developer. From classroom teacher to entrepreneur, she forged her own professional path by transferring her teaching expertise to becoming a keynote speaker. For two decades she has educated, empowered, and enriched people from all walks of life through her teachings, speeches, and online content. Dupé is now recognized as one of the top motivational influencers and the leading authority for curriculum and online course development.

However, her success came from misfortune. Dupé shares her story on how she survived a life-threatening medical condition by tapping into her greatest superpower: an unwavering ability to conquer adversity, while leading through change — and how you can do it too.

www.DupeAleru.com
www.facebook.com/DupeAleru
www.instagram.com/DupeAleru
www.linkedin.com/in/DupeAleru

IS COACHING YOUR CALLING?

HOW TO LEVERAGE COACHING TO BECOME A BOSS

TIFFANY BETHEA

I never wanted to be a coach. Like seriously, I was completely disinterested in being a coach or at least being called one. It was seemingly becoming a very trendy word and I tend to go in the opposite direction of the crowd. It was honestly to the point where when I first heard my clients refer to me as their coach, my stomach would turn. I was so uncomfortable. But that was until I had my great epiphany. That was 2013.

Now I consider it an honor and a pleasure to be a coach. It is immensely fulfilling to have an upfront seat to watch people tap into and maximize their potential. I do not take it lightly that I am invited into a very personal space with my clients to be a voice in their ears. Coaching is a calling, one that I am so glad I answered.

In 2016, I founded Kingdomboss. I have to tell you Kingdomboss is not a business; it is a God assignment. It is an answer to my call to coach. Through this brand, I combine faith and business to help authors, speakers, and entrepreneurs create profitable, Christ-centered brands. It is a deeply personal and intimate journey where I consider myself a midwife as my clients give birth to greater in their businesses and lives. I have prayed with my clients. I have cried with my clients. I have laughed with my clients. I have fussed at my clients. I have celebrated with my clients. Eventually, my clients become family. Each person I work with is assigned to me. We win together!

What exactly is coaching? I want to make sure that we are working from the same frame of reference in terms of what it actually is and not just in the context of how people portray it. Coaching is a special relationship whereby the coach helps an individual to bridge the gap between where they are and where they desire to be in a particular area of their life. This may include life coaching, business coaching, career coaching, and relationship coaching to name a few. One important aspect of coaching is tapping into untapped potential. Often coaching focuses more on helping people to implement what they already know versus teaching new information.

I want you to imagine an athletic coach. Picture the basketball game. Can you see it? Can you see the court? Can you see the players? Typically, during the game, the coach can be seen in a variety of roles. At times they are silently watching from the sidelines observing how their players are implementing what has been taught. Other times they can be seen in a huddle reminding them of strategy, motivating them, and pushing them towards the win. And some of my favorite moments are when they are seen yelling and screaming to their players. All of these can be likened to the role of a coach. There will be times when you are working with a client and quietly observing their words or watching how they handle a situation. Other times you have to be the person in their ear encouraging them on what they can do, reminding them of their why, reminding them of the goal ahead, imploring them not to focus on the distractions. Other times you have to exhibit tough love and have in your face conversations to wake them up in order to move them into action.

Case and point. Early on as I was still finding my way as a coach, I had a client who I was helping to build her brand from scratch. This project included publishing her first book. She was a dream client! I absolutely loved working with her. Each session she showed up prepared, focused, and ready to implement. Each time we spoke she had done what was asked and she built an incredible brand that is rocking to this day.

During one particular session, we both showed up and it was a little different than the others. She was not in the normal energy I was used to. I had given her the assignment of writing her book outline and she had not completed it. This was a first. Up until this point I had not used tough love with her because it had not been necessary. But this time was different.

I asked her why she had not gotten the outline done and she gave me a list of excuses. I could easily decipher that these were not valid reasons and definitely not enough to keep from her completing her assignment. I felt something in me rise that had not happened yet. I told her flat out that she had given me a list of excuses that did not hold any weight. I told her that the real bottom line was that she was afraid and that she had to decide whether or not she really wanted to do this. I exhorted her that until she made a firm decision, she would continue to find excuses.

She looked at me in a manner that said I had hit a nerve. She was not upset with me, but she definitely felt a way. I know she was not used to that tone from me. She acknowledged that she could have pushed harder. I prayed with her as usual and we ended the session.

Can you guess what happened during our next session? She had not only written the outline, but she had also completed the entire book!

I could not believe it. But it was one of the first times I truly understood the power of the coaching relationship. That book was locked up inside of her. Who knows how long it would have stayed locked up without the encouragement and accountability of a coach.

I am using this illustration to help you understand the power of the coaching relationship. It is truly a calling. It is a commitment to go beyond the surface of your client into the deep to pull out of them the treasure that is within. It can be a messy journey, but it always yields beautiful results.

Coaching is a much deeper dive and commitment than other types of speaking. Think about it. The emcee, the keynote speaker, the motivational speaker, the trainer you may never see again after they deliver their talk. Those types of speaking tend to be a short-term relationship between the speaker and audience member. And for that reason, I know people who are disinterested in coaching. Their preference is the short-term exchange. This is something you must seriously consider when deciding to add coaching to your speaker roster. Do you desire short-term exchanges, or do you desire to stick around and go deeper with your audience? I know that I am called to coach because I do not enjoy the short-term exchange nearly as much as my coaching relationships.

Are you feeling the calling to coaching? Are you a speaker that is considering creating a coaching program? How can you tell if you will be a good coach? Here are a few traits that make a great coach:

- Active listener
- Empathic and encouraging
- Enjoy helping people
- Ability to build rapport and trust
- Ability to ask the right questions
- Comfortable extending tough love
- Does not feel pressure to have the answer rather than discover the answer
- Enjoy giving step by step instructions

How can you leverage speaking to establish yourself as a coach? One thing you must understand is that the coaching relationship requires a lot of trust. Your potential clients need to establish trust not only in your subject matter expertise, but also in you as the person guiding them on their journey. They must feel safe to open up about where they truly are now and the grandeur of where they desire to go. Speaking engagements can serve as a great source of lead generation for coaching clients. It gives you an opportunity to make a powerful connection and first impression.

If you are thinking of answering the call to coach here are a few ways to get started:

1. Get clear on who your audience is and the problem they are experiencing. What solution will you provide them with?

2. Craft a program that is designed to take participants on a thorough journey. The length of the program should carefully consider how long it takes for them to see transformation in the selected area. Deeper healing and more intense areas may require longer programs.

3. Use your speaking platform to get in front of qualified leads for your program. Allow your talk to make a powerful first impression. Share your own experience with the transformation journey you want to invite them to take. How were you able to make the change? How will you help them make the change?

4. Consider starting with a beta-test. When creating any new program, you are not 100% sure of its effectiveness. Invite participants to take part at a reduced price and give feedback so that you can

tweak and perfect before you take it to the market. One huge benefit of this is that when you debut the program you will already have testimonials and experience that will draw potential clients.

Coaching is a calling. It is a special relationship where you are invited into a personal space for the sole purpose of creating a solution where there is a problem. Coaching is not for everyone. But for all of us who answer the call, it is a deeply rewarding and lucrative opportunity to serve mankind. If you sense the calling, I highly encourage you to answer. I answered my call one day and I have never looked back.

Tiffany Bethea

Tiffany Bethea is a bestselling author, international speaker, trained coach and consultant, ordained minister and mompreneur. She is the founder of Kingdomboss through which she has provided a space for Christian entrepreneurs to build profitable, Christ-centered brands. Through the signature program Kingdomboss Society new and emerging authors, speakers, and entrepreneurs' mastermind with other believers in business and gain the accountability, resources, and strategy they need to be successful. She is also a spiritual teacher and coach who works with millennials on upgrading from their counterfeit existence to truly living the life God has predestined for them. She is passionate about helping people discover their true identity and maximize their potential.

www.tiffanybethea.com
@tiffanylbethea on all platforms

NEW PAYMENT RECEIVED!

HOW TO CREATE SIZZLING SALES COPY FOR YOUR SOLUTIONS

APRYL BEVERLY

Remember the excitement that raced through your veins whenever you would get that notorious message from AOL, "you've got mail"?

Well, you are going to feel it again. Only now, the message is going to be from PayPal, Stripe Apple Pay and so on. And they are ALL going to scream: "You've got money!" Whether you have struggled to connect with your community of prospects in the past or you are just starting out, I want you to know that you have finally found the one place created for ambitious goal seekers – by ambitious goal seekers – looking to answer that nagging question:

"Why am I posting on social media, sending out emails, writing pitch proposals, and otherwise marketing myself nonstop and NOT seeing more money?"

All entrepreneurs – whether you are a speaker, business coach, photographer, or other type of genius service provider – are either growing or dying. And because there is truly no in between (for example, you cannot be "half-dead" or "almost growing"), you are in the midst of an incredible opportunity to soar (or sink) depending on how well you can connect with your audience. If you apply the following quick tips when you write your next piece of sales copy, not only will it sizzle, BUT it will snap by propelling folks to smack the buy button™.

THE "MIGHTY 5" QUICK TIPS FOR CRAFTING COPY THAT SIZZLES AND SELLS

Before we get to the Mighty 5, let's start with a straight-up-no-chaser definition of copywriting and copy:

Copywriting is the art of writing in a way that propels people to act – be it to buy, download, call, and so on.

Copywriting not only gets folks to smack the buy button when you are "NOT in the room," but it also serves your audience in a way that propels them to take a specific action. How, you ask? Copywriting is the act of writing to pierce the hearts of your peeps, so they do what YOU want them to do – download your freebie, register for your webinar, enroll in your course, or simply open your email.

In short, copywriting is the act of producing content used for the purpose of advertising, marketing, and sales. This type of text, known as copy, is also used to raise brand awareness and persuade the ideal client to part with their money or take some other desired action – download your free eBook, participate in your webinar, register for your email list.

Speak Up!

Do you still want to craft a smokin' hot sales message that excites, engages, and propels the RIGHT people to smack you upside the head with their wallets? These Mighty 5 quick tips will teach you how to do exactly that:

Quick Tip #1 – Tingle Spines and Curl Toes

Using emotion in your writing is the KEY to crafting copy that sizzles and sells. Maya Angelou says that people never forget how you make them feel. Emotional appeal is why we desire things, and it is why we take action to get the things we want.

"Desire" is an emotional impulse. The trick to writing with emotion is crafting messages that trigger the right emotion in your audience. What you do not want to do is have your audience crying all over every landing page you publish or sending people into a deep dark depression where they convince themselves they cannot change their existing situation – even with your help.

INSTEAD, you want to walk the fine line between pain and hope by reiterating your buyer's pain and right before they feel all hope is lost, present them with your product or service as the solution.

After all, Maya Angelou says it best:

"People will forget what you said, people will forget what you did, but people will never forget how you made them feel."

Quick Tip #2 – Do Not Just Educate … ENTERTAIN

Delivery is critical whether you are educating your audience from the stage or asking them to engage with your written copy. If you deliver your offer in a boring way, your audience will be bored. However, if you are amped up and excited about serving people with your incredible offer, they will feed into that and they will be excited too.

Please know that entertaining your audience is NOT about being someone other than yourself. It is about being ALL of you. And a great way to educate and entertain at the same time is through storytelling.

Copywriters use stories all the time because they are a powerful way to sell. They can influence sympathy and encourage donations. They can cause a revolution or protest. They can provoke a response. And most importantly for you, they can sell. The key to storytelling is delivering stories that not only engage your audience but to also hit your buyers' pain points and paint a picture not only of their struggles, but also of what life will be like for them after they invest in your solution.

Quick Tip #3 – Sell the Steak and the Sizzle

Most marketers will tell you to sell the benefits, not the steak. And to put it plainly… that is simply not an effective way to get people to buy into your solution. Why? Because while the sizzle is exciting and thrilling, buyers still want the actual steak.

For example, how would you feel if you ordered a steak at your favorite restaurant and instead of a hot, juicy steak, the waiter brought a recorder that allowed you to listen to the steak as it sizzled on the plate in the kitchen? LOL

Yes, the benefits are important and every feature of your product or service should be tied to a specific feature, but you cannot forget to also sell the features by letting people know exactly what they expect from investing in your solutions.

Quick Tip #4 – Talk to Yourself

Want to write sales copy that leaps off the page and pierces the hearts of your prospects? Learn how to love talking to yourself. Great copy is conversational. This means if you want to connect with your audience, you have to master the art of having a conversation in writing.

Deliver your words in the way you speak in real life. Your authentic voice will engage readers instead of driving them away with impersonal, techie talk. The bottom line is this: If you do not hear yourself talking when you write, you are not doing it right.

Quick Tip #5 – Pitch with a Purpose

Every piece of content you share on social media, from the stage, at networking events and via other marketing channels should be tied to at least one of these core business goals: (1) build brand awareness; (2) connect on a deeper level with your community; or, (3) straight-up sell your solutions.

If you cannot share a sales or marketing message with one of those core purposes, then you need to rethink what you plan to share, because PITCHING WITH A PURPOSE is critical in helping you receive that gloriously delicious message of "you've got money"!

****

And there you have it, the Mighty 5 quick tips to creating sales copy that not only sizzles, but also sells! In closing, please know a smokin' hot, compelling piece of copy can skyrocket brand awareness, create a loyal community of buyers, boost revenue and position you to serve more of the people who need you most.

While receiving that "new payment received" alert is essential to your longevity as an entrepreneur, mastering the art of crafting sizzling copy will not only keep the money flowing but it will constantly drive a fresh pile of raving fans your way. And that right there is the key to unimaginable, sustainable success in this wild and crazy world of entrepreneurship.

APRYL BEVERLY

Apryl Beverly crafts compelling copy that has generated over $20 million in revenue for B2B solo entrepreneurs, small business owners and some of the country's top brands.

Known for her "tell-it-like-it-is" writing style, she has earned a variety of awards and recognitions including hitting the Amazon Best Seller's List in 3 categories just 24 hours after releasing her first book, Shots Fired! How to Write Copy that Pierces Hearts (And Opens Wallets).

Her second book, F.A.S.T. Money! The Easy Way to use Facebook Ads to Hook Smokin' Hot Leads shot to the No. 1 spot on Amazon's Best Seller's List two days before its official release. Apryl's work has also been featured in The Huffington Post, YFS Magazine, and other notable online and print publications.

Apryl brings 18 years of experience in copywriting, marketing communications and proposal writing to her role as CEO of BAAB Writing and Marketing Services.

She is also the founder of Word Stylistz™, the first woman-owned flat rate copywriting service agency catering to the unique needs of small business owners and entrepreneurs who serve diverse audiences.

She is a graduate of The Ohio State University in Journalism and the University of Phoenix in Master of Business Administration in Marketing.

Visit stylemywords.co to experience her spine-tingling sentence slinging skills for yourself.

www.facebook.com/baabwriting
www.instagram.com/baabwriting
www.linkedin.com/company/baabwriting

PITCH YOUR WAY TO PROFIT!
FUNDING YOUR BUSINESS THROUGH PITCH COMPETITIONS
QUINN CONYERS

I have won $34,000 speaking about my business in 22 minutes!

This was not all at once, but after I did the math and calculated the time, that is the end result!

I am an entrepreneur who uses speaking to fund my bag business, the Purse Paparazzi.

I have been speaking professionally since college. I have been a full-time entrepreneur since 2015 and quickly learned that having a great product or awesome service does not equal instant sales.

If you are not able to speak about your business in a way that is clear, concise, and compelling you are losing money every time!

This chapter is specifically for speakers who are also entrepreneurs.

I personally believe that speaking must be included in your business as a revenue stream, marketing strategy, or funding source.

For the purpose of this book, I will focus on how to use speaking as a funding strategy to expand your business.

Speaking also known as pitching in this context shows up big in your business. When people ask, "What do you do"? Your response can help or hurt your business.

A common speech many entrepreneurs are familiar with is called the "Elevator Pitch." It is called this because the idea is you should be able to explain what you do to someone in the amount of time it takes you to ride from the ground floor up to the penthouse in an elevator. (This usually is 30-60 seconds)

This idea of an elevator pitch has been remixed in the business world adding a competition component that is becoming wildly popular.

With business reality TV shows like Shark Tank, many entrepreneurs are getting more clever and creative on how they speak about their business.

This is exactly what I have done!

Speak Up!

Through participating in business pitch competitions, I have leveraged my speaking abilities to impress investors and WIN!

If you are new to the concept of business pitch competitions, get excited!

I am about to show how to speak and fund your business at the same time.

Business pitch competitions are when entrepreneurs compete by giving their best elevator pitch in hopes of winning cash and or prizes to expand their enterprise.

Prize money can be anywhere from a few hundred dollars to millions!

The exposure and publicity from pitching in competitions is priceless, regardless if you take home the grand prize!

Personally, I have won $34,000 in various pitch competitions. However, the people I have met along the way and the relationships I have formed are worth much more than that.

I have pitched and made it to the 2nd round of Shark Tank three times, pitched my product to HSN and appeared on the Entrepreneurs Elevator Pitch TV Show.

I was a finalist for the Black Enterprise Magazine annual Pitch Competition, placed 3rd in the National Urban League Pitch Competition and received 3 out of 4 golden tickets in a pitch competition hosted by the Hip Hop Film Festival in Harlem, New York. Essence Magazine chose me as a "brand" they wanted to work with, and I got to be a vendor at their annual Essence Street Style event!

Speaking about my business in pitch competitions have opened up so many doors for me as a speaker and entrepreneur.

I am proud to have become a "Business Pitch Champion" but honestly, I have lost more competitions than I have won. I have flown to cities unsure what to say when 60 seconds and $10,000 was on the line and that is why I have made it my mission to help other entrepreneurs use their voice to fund their business.

Based on my experience speaking and pitching, there a few things you need to consider if you want to Pitch Your Way to funding.

First, you have to be able to find these competitions. The three platforms I use to find my competitions are Google, Eventbrite, and Instagram. By using simple keyword searches such as "business pitch competition" coupled with my city or state, all types of competitions pop up.

Next, you need to be aware of the business pitch application process.

You cannot just show up and pitch. You have to apply, get notified, and selected to pitch. The process usually involves three easy steps. First, you must apply. This includes answering questions about your business.

Questions can include anything from your niche, your advantage in the marketplace and sales from the previous year. Some applications require or have an optional video submission. Always do the video! Investors want to see your passion for your product or service in person. Make sure you adhere to the video time limits. Most videos submissions are short (60 seconds is normal). They usually want you to describe your business and share how you will use the money if you win.

After you submit your video and application, they will let you know either way if you have been selected to pitch. That is when the real fun begins! They will email you everything you need to do to properly prepare for the competition. If you are not selected to pitch, it is OK. The more you enter, the more chances you have to win and get exposure for your business.

Lastly, you need a powerful elevator pitch that will impress investors and increase your chances of winning. This is where YOU shine as a speaker!

I am confident that those who are speakers have a slight advantage when pitching.

Your business pitch should be clear, concise, compelling, and delivered with confidence. Investors are equally excited about your product as they are about your passion for it. Speaking about your business in competitions is very different from a keynote, panelist, or workshop leader.

Your time is short (Usually 30 seconds to 2 minutes) followed by Questions and Answers. Many of the questions asked would be similar to the questions you answered in the application.

Each competition is not created equal so reading the rules and regulations for each competition will be in your best interest.

When you are pitching, a panel of investors will choose the winner, or the LIVE audience will. Sometimes it is a combination of both. Again, read the contest rules so you are clear.

The prizes of these competitions are worthwhile! You can win cash and all sorts of business prizes and services. I have seen office space, mentorship, and $100,000 been awarded in these competitions.

I have won cash, a printer, and networking opportunities I could not afford on my own. Speaking about my business has truly been rewarding and lucrative beyond the financial incentives.

As you prepare to speak about your business in pitch competitions, I want to share with you my P.I.T.C.H. method that I have used to pitch my way to profit.

P: Presentation

What you wear and how you deliver your pitch matters. 93% of all communication is non-verbal. Before you open your mouth, people are judging you from the stage. Make sure you wear clothes that align with your brand and that display you are comfortable and confident. If you are not a suit and tie type of guy or girl do not wear one when you pitch.

Be sure your excitement and passion for your business are evident. If you are not excited about your business neither will the audience or judges be. This energy has to come through in your presentation at all times.

I: Investment Ask

When pitching, the prize money will be known up front or you can ask for the amount you need. Either way always asks for the amount of money you need and include how you will use the funds.

T: Twist

Investors also known as judges are looking for innovation, not a brand-new business idea. You must include what makes your business different, special, or unique. What is YOUR twist or competitive advantage?

C: Cash

Similar to shows like Shark Tank, some but not all competitions want to know how much money you have already made. This can include money you made year to date or over the lifespan of your company. The higher the amount of the prize money, the more they will want to know your sales and sale history. The lower the amount, I would say under $10,000, your sales history is not as important.

H: Hire Help

If you know you need help developing and delivering a pitch hire help! You can take a class or invest in pitch a session. I have personally done all of these. I have taken pitch classes in Washington DC and New York. I also offer workshops and pitch strategy sessions myself. There is no need to pitch alone. Your business can be funded in 60 seconds or less. Be sure to invest in yourself so when you take the stage you are ready to pitch your way to funding.

Pitching is a valuable skill that speakers can utilize to fund their business. With proper preparation you too can Pitch Your Way to Profit.

QUINN CONYERS

Quinn Conyers is a Business Pitch Champion! She has personally used speaking as a strategy to fund her bag business the Purse Paparazzi.

To date, she has won $34,000 in business pitch competitions. She has also made it to the 2nd round of Shark Tank 3 times, pitched her product to HSN and has appeared on the Entrepreneurs Elevator Pitch TV Show.

Quinn is now helping other entrepreneurs who are also speakers use their voice to fund their business!

She does this by helping them develop and deliver a powerful elevator pitch so every time they open their mouth, they make money.

Quinn's accomplishments have allowed her to appear in Essence, Black Enterprise, and Young Money Magazines. On a local level, she has been featured on Fox 5 News in Washington DC, Bmore Lifestyle TV, and a host of newspapers.

Quinn has spoken at numerous conferences and hosts her own workshops and seminars teaching expert entrepreneurs how to craft a compelling business pitch.

Quinn's experience as a speaker coupled with her pitching expertise makes her an in-demand keynote speaker and workshop facilitator.

She has earned her bachelor's degree from West Chester University in PA and a master's from Howard University in Washington DC.

Quinn currently resides in Maryland with her husband and 2 sons.

To book Quinn as a Speaker
Visit www.QuinnConyers.com and follow her on social media @QuinnConyers

www.facebook.com/quinnconyers
www.instagram.com/quinn.conyers
www.linkedin.com/in/quinnconyers

TIRED OF WAITING TO GET BOOKED?

UNLOCK THE POWER OF HOSTING LIVE EVENTS

MOTHYNA JAMES-BRIGHTFUL

Hosting your own event strengthens your presence as an expert in your field and increases your influence factor with your ideal audience. Anyone who tells you that live events are dead hasn't paid much attention to some of the largest and most profitable corporations in the world. Google, Exxon, Apple, and Amazon all host multiple live events each year. In this chapter, when we say "live" event we are discussing an in-person experience where you meet with your potential clients face-to-face. Why would some of the largest corporations in the world still meet face to face with potential buyers, partners, and clients? Because it makes cents. Live events are profitable.

Please note we are not saying that online webinars are not profitable or offer several benefits, however, the reality is connecting in person often has a longer and deeper impact. Humans crave connection and intimacy. It builds significant trust and likeability. And when I like and trust you, I am willing to be influenced by you.

Live events help you build your connection with your community. Online events and programs have value. They generate income, but live events are where you pull it all together. Guess what else! Most of the largest names in the speaking industry host their own live events. Eric Thomas, Brian Tracy, Lisa Nichols, Robin Sharma, and Tony Robbins all host their own events. Success leaves clues and it is up to us to pick them up and implement for our own success.

Over the course of my career, I have hosted various types of events and I have been honored to work behind the scenes at some major programs. Through volunteering for events such as Speak and Write to Make Millions, The eWoman Network Entrepreneur Conference and non-profit events like End Violence Against Women International Conference, I have learned key strategies to generate impact and influence with my own events. Through the skills and strategies included here, my one-day free local conference became an international women's organization, whose multi-day annual event repeatedly attracts women from around the world.

Everything you read over the next several pages can be applied to any type of event. Let's work together to propel your next event experience to mastery. As you get your aha's today, tap into the community and share your learning using the hashtag #stageready.

Currently, I plan multi-day events, with over 800 registrants including multiple vendors and speakers. However, the days of events where no one showed up or there were just eight people, are never too far from my mind. As an event producer, we often think once we have hosted a successful event then they will all be amazing from then on. Your event success is not going be linear. It will have ups and downs, which is how success truly looks. Embrace that your journey is going to be a rollercoaster and give yourself permission to breathe. After that repeat your wins, learn from your errors and adjust.

There are many reasons why we believe our events fail. Does any of this sound familiar? *I do not have any money. I do not have a team to help me. Not enough people registered.* These are some real challenges, yet most events fail before they ever begin, because 90% of people who have an event idea, never carry it out. You may have considered an idea for years and you have not done it yet. It feels like a failure because you have not acted. Let's recommit and focus on how to make your next event whether it is your first or 50th an absolute success.

Top 5 Secrets to Transform Your Next Live Event

Start with the end in mind by answering the question, what is your intention for hosting this event. Visualizing the experience from beginning to end makes planning for success easier. How does it smell? What does it feel like in the space? How do I define my program as a success? Very rarely, is it based on the number of attendees or the amount of money generated. Honestly, the transformation that we are seeking has to do with the individuals that show up.

Building an audience is about the persons that need what you offer in the world. Consider the 30/30/30/10 equation to attract your ideal audience. Thirty percent of your ideal audience is aware they have a problem but are not ready to act to solve that problem. Approximately, 30% is aware they have a problem that needs to be fixed but are determined to fix it later. The next 30% are not aware they have a problem. Ninety percent of your ideal audience are not looking for you. That leaves approximately 10% actively looking for and open to the solution you provide. How do you build an audience with that? If you activate the 30% that are delaying solving their problem and the 30% unaware, they have a problem that you solve, how would that change your engagement? You are now working on attracting nearly 70 percent of your ideal audience. Find a way to reach the three segments of people that are not focused on you within the marketing for your event.

Create an experience. What is your pink elephant? Once you get them in the room, what is going to make them want to come back? What about your experience will have everyone saying, "oh my gosh" and telling everyone else about? It does not have to be a physical product. It can be an intangible experience. The ultimate goal is to create raving reviews and repeat business. Determine what kind of experience you want your ideal attendee to have and start building it before they enter the room. Every interaction before the event flows with the in-room and post-event experience.

Set the tone. The tone delivers the intention for the event through your marketing efforts. Does your pre-event marketing, videos, flyers, calls, webinars, emails etc. bring the "in the room" promise? If you have followed the strategies so far but miss out on this next step, you will struggle to see the benefit of live events. Training your staff, volunteers, and vendors on the tone of the event prior to the day is critical. The goal is to ensure that your event team matches the energy you have created through your previous efforts. This requires advanced training on the details, which is the last strategy in this section.

Do not hold all the cards. For approximately 10 years, my co-founder and I built a system where everyone had to come to us for even the smallest problem. During this time, we rarely if ever, spoke on stage. Instead, we built events which showcased other experts. The year we shared our expertise from the main stage, our ideal audience literally said, "I want more of you." Honoring this request shifted our profit and impact. Being stage ready meant we could no longer hold all the cards. We needed to duplicate two people into 25! If everyone is coming to you for all the answers, there is no way that you can clear your mind enough to deliver from the stage.

What To Do First

If you are just getting started and need to know what to do first, this section is for you.

What is the purpose and impact of your event? This answer is the guide to the experience you are creating. The clearer you become, the greater your ability to achieve the goal. In order to make an impact, you want to make sure that your team is 110% committed to the purpose and the impact.

Choose your tribe. Free community-based events may not have the same clientele as events with a fee. Knowing whom you desire to attend is the only truly powerful way to plan for success. Who are they? What are their psycho and demo graphics?

Event style. A seminar has a different connotation than a retreat. The type of the event determines your set up. Does this event need 60 8ft tables with 300 chairs, 4 rooms, a stage, sound system, electricity, etc.? Or do you need beach towels, a cabana, and ten wine glasses? Which type of event is going to serve the program plan best?

Selecting the venue. Understand which type of space will allow you and your team to deliver the best experience for the attendees. For example, a venue that has exposed brick and six-foot windows is different from a venue that has all white walls and no windows. These environments deliver two different types of experiences. The venue selection should be based on the purpose and impact you want to deliver and how it all comes together.

Scheduling. Consider events your ideal audience may attend and determine if there are any major conflicts. Is there a similar event in the vicinity that typically happens around the same time? Let's say you want to host a festival-style event for authors in Baltimore, Maryland. Do not plan it for September. Why? One of the largest book author festivals in the country happens in Baltimore each September. Why try and compete? Strategically, host your event 30-45 days after that event and use that book festival as a marketing opportunity to reach an ideal audience.

A Note on Marketing...

We are all in the business of the 3M's, marketing, marketing, marketing. If you want your message, to reach the masses, you must do the marketing. Is the message clear, specific, and laser focused? How can your message reach your ideal audience? Where do they hang out, eat, learn, or play? The clearer it is defined, the more successful the goal.

Spending and Profit Plan

If you do not plan for profit, there will be no profit. The event budget is the spending and profit plan. A truly profitable plan considers the cost per person and determines what to sell before, after, and during the event. Crowdfunding, social media, and other online fundraising platforms are resources to consider. Sponsorship is one way to generate funds. There are two popular types of sponsorship in-kind and fiscal. Fiscal is often a monetary check. In-kind is generally a donation of products or service. Note, it can take months or even years to nurture a sponsor, plan accordingly. It is more attractive to offer year-round access to your community vs solo event sponsorship. Ticket sales are a pre-event profit generator. During the event products, services, joint-venture partners are all funding sources. Design your post-event strategy with sales in mind. Offer services and products for sale through your follow-up strategy.

Too many speakers focus on finding stages that someone else has built. However, we have established that some of the most prominent figures in any industry often host their own events. The goal is to have you stage ready. Mastering the ability to stand on the stage and have people tune into your every single word. I firmly believe that when people enjoy what they are learning, they engage more, spend more, and refer you more. As a stage ready speaker, you can dominate your niche through your own events, with high engagement and engagement sells.

MOTHYNA JAMES-BRIGHTFUL

 Mothyna James-Brightful is described as "energetic, passionate and inspirational" by audiences. A professional public speaker for over 14 years, she has spent nearly 50,000 hours speaking. Sister Mothyna has honored speaking requests at numerous conferences, community programs and schools. In recognition of her works, she has appeared in publications such as The Daily Record, Ebony Magazine, Be What I Want to Be Magazine and The Afro-American Newspapers. She is an Amazon Bestselling author and co-founder of Heal a Woman to Heal a Nation, Inc. Throughout her career, she has planned and executed countless events which elevated her platform and created an opportunity for others to do the same. Her stages have welcomed speakers such as Harriette Cole, Cheryl Woods, African Miranda, Dr. Brenda Green and so many more. Sister Mothyna holds a bachelor's degree in journalism from Morgan State University and a master's in human service administration from The University of Baltimore.

@mothyna

WHY JUMP ON A PLANE?
HOW TO WIN WITH WEBINARS
DEKESHA WILLIAMS

I was able to grow a sustainable business from the comfort of my own home. Now my story is a little different considering I lost the same job twice. We received an email on January 11, 2010, that our company had ceased operations. So, for about four months, I was unemployed and attempting to collect unemployment. Within those four months, they called us back to open over 164 locations across the United States. Honestly, there was something about the second time around that did not sit very well with me.

The morning of August 24, 2011, I turned in my pink slip and I went on a leave of absence. I am still on that leave of absence. #LongestLeaveEver. At that moment, I reevaluated everything that was important to me. I knew that being present for my children meant everything to me. For the past 1,286 days, I have been able to see both my daughter and my son get on and off the bus, since kindergarten and the sixth grade.

I think the opportunity to have memories or create memories is important to me. I wanted to create a profitable business that would allow me to continue being present for my family. Around seven and a half years ago, I was not in a position to travel and bounce around the country attending conferences on a weekly basis. I was spending my life in the airport as a district manager for 13 locations over five states. Living my life out of a suitcase with constant traveling defeated the purpose of me going on a leave of absence to be home and available for my children. This was the main reason that I decided to finally walk away from my corporate job.

I was introduced to the technology of webinars and it has been the vehicle of choice that enables me to get my message to the masses. Throughout the last four and a half years, I have studied the ins and outs of webinars including how to drive traffic to webinars, how to make sales, and how to have sales conversations on a webinar. I started teaching clients who were serious about building an online business and willing to pay $15,000 to $25,000. I taught them how to create a webinar sequence that will bring people into the entry point of the sequence where there is an attraction phase, followed by engaging and nurturing the relationship which ultimately invites them into a webinar where you offer them the opportunity to work with you. I taught that system for four and a half years. I am a person that believes in theory. I believe in tried, true, and tested. Even though I taught those systems, it was still a theory because it had not worked for me. I taught it to clients, but it was still theoretical in my mind because it was not working in my business.

I was showing other people how to work it in their business and made up my mind that I was going to prove that what I was teaching was not hypothetical and it was not theoretical. It is factual that people can have five-figure and six-figure launches from webinars and they do not need to leave their home. There are some people who have had a six-figure launch profit from webinars and they are not even showing up live. These are called automated webinars.

In the last few years, I have tested 12 ways to get people to show up and register for your webinar. I have tested how to increase your show rate from the industry standard of 20% to 30, 40, and sometimes 50%. I have tested getting anywhere from a 5, 10 to 15% closing ratio on webinars and then closing another 15% in the follow-up process.

There are a few items that you will need to begin using webinars in your business:

- **Email Marketing System** - An email marketing system is a vehicle that allows you to collect names and emails when people register for your webinar. This is where you start to build a list of prospective buyers who are truly interested in your product and/or services.

- **Webinar Software** – There is a plethora of webinar software available to entrepreneurs seeking to utilize them in their business. We are very specific about utilizing a webinar software because of the functionalities such as automation. Be mindful to look for software that allows you to run on-demand/automated webinars while allowing you to provide relevant information at the convenience of the end user. The most popular platforms available are Webinar Jam, EverWebinar, and Easy Webinar.

- **Signature Presentation** - This is the message that you are presenting to the masses. Remember speaking is about providing value to the end user and you are still able to impact lives via online digital events i.e. webinars. You must create a compelling message to prompt audience participation. Be prepared with a signature offer to invite prospects to work with you.

If you have never hosted a webinar or you are not sure of where to start, I am sharing a free resource, The Webinar Checklist, to provide you a guide to host your first online presentation. Download the free resource at http://bit.ly/2iP0jjP

Now that I have seen the same results in my business as my clients have, profitable webinar success is no longer theoretical for me. I don't have to return to the corporate world and spend countless hours going through TSA or attempting to get a TSA pre-approval so that I can get through the airport faster. I don't have to get up at 3:00 in the morning to be at the airport to catch a 4:00 am flight and then try to return home to my kids on the same evening or the next day. To be quite honest with you, when I am booked now, I feel guilty about leaving my kids even though they are a lot older now. I am in a position to make it work for me. It has been a great journey of testing what used to be theoretical in my mind and seeing it evolve into five-figure launches from the comfort of my home.

I invite you to learn more about using webinars in your business by visiting www.TheWebinarSuccessBlueprint.com

This is DeKesha Williams, Your Virtual COO

Remember to be passionate, be purposeful, but more importantly, be profitable.

DEKESHA WILLIAMS

 As a single mom of two, often times it was hard to just up and travel to all of the conferences happening across the country. I would always feel guilty about leaving my kids at home especially when trying to find someone to stay home with them. They love being at home and I would feel guilty about removing them from their element.

I would always refer back to the fact that I left corporate America in 2011 to be present for my children. To jump on planes, trains and travel across the country defeated the purpose of staying home to present with my kids.

Then I found this software that allowed me to teach, train and facilitate from the comfort of my own home.

Let me help you develop a new revenue stream using webinars.

www.TheWebinarChallenge.com
www.facebook.com/dekesha
www.instagram.com/de_kesha

PRODUCING MULTIPLE PATHS TO PROFIT!
CREATING MULTIPLE STREAMS OF INCOME FOR LONG-TERM SUCCESS
LAKESHA WOMACK

As a professional speaker, it is imperative that you create multiple streams of income to help sustain your business. Throughout this book, there are strategies to help make this a reality. It can be tempting to think that you do not need to implement any of these strategies because you are anticipating an influx of clients paying your full fee. That is definitely the goal in our industry but not the guarantee.

A few things to consider when creating multiple revenue streams…

- ***The path that you invest the most in will probably yield the most results.*** The strategies you choose to implement should enhance your brand's platform, help to increase your visibility among your target audience, and add value to the lessons promoted in your speaking. Do not try to do everything at once but focus on a few things to do really well.

- ***It takes money to make money.*** There are a lot of free tools that you can use but they often come with limitations. To get the full benefits of anything you are interested in pursuing, be willing to make some type of investment. Your business budget should include expenses that are a cost of doing business as well as revenue streams.

- ***Do not hesitate to outsource.*** If you are busy working a full-time job or do not have the time/skill set to execute one or more of the strategies that you feel will fit your brand's goals, hire help.

- ***Some months/seasons will be better for some streams than others.*** One of the benefits of planting multiple seeds is having a larger variety to harvest. As the author of ten books, a business consultant, leadership development facilitator, and brand designer; I may have more speaking engagements one month and more brand clients the next. By continuously promoting the different streams, my pipeline stays filled with work.

- ***Know your audience and your community.*** When you execute a strategy, your network should say, "yes, that makes sense" and not wonder where this idea came from.

- ***Create a strategic plan to understand how the strategies will fit into your plan or help you achieve your goals.*** People know when you are doing things or offering a product/service just to make money. You want to be sure you are solving a problem for your clients and not trying to hustle them out of their coins. Those strategies may work for a short term, but they are not sustainable. Your goal should be to build a long term, profitable business.

- ***Set goals.*** It is hard to know if a strategy is working if you do not have any metrics to measure it. Do some research to determine what is reasonable in your market so that you can set realistic goals. You should not expect to reach the goal immediately, rather build to the goal. For example, you want to host an event generating $50,000 in profit. You may need to start small and build your audience over 3-5 years to reach that goal.

Eleven Paths to Profits

Let's talk strategy. Again, all of these strategies are not for everyone and you may think of a different spin to add that will make the strategy unique to your brand. Use this list as a starting point. Think about your budget for each, resources (people and time) needed to execute, and your projected revenue to determine if it is actually, and not just emotionally, feasible for your brand.

1. **Write a book.** In all honesty, you probably will not make a lot of money from your book without a strong marketing strategy, but book sales create residual income. They also help to establish your credibility when booking speaking engagements as well as allowing you to make additional income at those engagements. If you speak to different audiences, it can be helpful to have a book tailored to each of your audiences so that when you are promoting your work, you can promote content that is relevant to the audience. Typically, promoting your book after a speaking engagement – live or virtual – will generate the most sales because you have established a

connection and credibility with your audience. *(See: I Wrote My Book, Now What?)*

2. **Host an event.** Events can be a great source of revenue if properly done. Many events fail because of poor planning and unrealistic projections. There are many factors to consider but your budget should be the first and foremost. How much will the event cost you? You should consider everything from the cost of the venue to the amount you plan to pay your speakers/panelists to the cost of napkins. From there, think about how much your attendees will pay to attend the event. It is best to look at similar events in your area to determine the market rate. Also factor in how many people attended those events and the caliber of speakers. If you are bringing in high profile speakers, you can charge a little more but make sure you have the marketing budget to support your event. Once you have decided on the price and have your budget, you can determine how many attendees you will need to break even. Every attendee after that is profit. If you cannot reasonably attain that number of attendees, you need to adjust your budget or your price. The goal is to not only host a great event that will make your attendees demand the next event but to also host a profitable event. *(See: Tired of Waiting to Get Booked)*

3. **Sell merchandise.** Before setting up your online store, think about what makes sense to offer to your network. Almost everyone wants to start with mugs, tee shirts, and journals but you need to ask yourself, realistically, what would make someone buy my product over the million other items in the market. Create a focus group to ask what they like and do not

like about the product, how much they would be willing to pay, and who they think the target audience is. Do not take their responses personally but take them seriously. Also, seek out dropshipping companies that will allow you to place orders as you receive them rather than maintaining an inventory. This reduces your initial investment and increases your profitability.

4. **Teach online.** Sharing your knowledge with your audience through online courses can be profitable because many people are forgoing traditional advanced degrees to attain the specialized knowledge needed from industry leaders. Ensure your course is truly adding value to your attendees and is not being used solely for lead generation to sell additional products. *(See: Cashing in on Courses!)*

5. **Become a coach or consultant.** In addition to group training and presenting from the stage, there are many people who see the value in working with you one-on-one. Understand your gifts in this area, develop a process for working with clients, and start with a smart group to develop your program. *(See: Is Coaching Your Calling?)*

6. **Allow ads on your site.** This can be a great source of passive income because the ads work for themselves, but you want to be careful about placement so that the content of your site does not get lost in advertisements. You may want to have a banner or footer ad or side ads promoting products/services that are complementary to your business. You can use a service like Google ad sense which may pay you based on clicks or impressions or you can also sell

ads to businesses/brands in your network and charge upfront. Before executing this strategy, review the analytics of your site to determine if you have the traffic to make your site attractive to advertisers.

7. **Create a community.** Develop a members-only section of your website where persons who pay a monthly fee can access specialized content from you. This content often includes your online courses, video tutorials, and the ability to network privately with other like-minded individuals. I suggest testing your market to determine the fee so that you can reduce cancellation rates, especially if it will be a monthly charge.

8. **Develop a referral network.** As an influencer with a strong network, you may find that your community consistently needs the services of professionals in your network. Consider working with that professional to provide you with a referral bonus for clients you are referring to them. I have several of these arrangements and typically pay around 10% for referrals. I highly recommend having worked with or having an intimate knowledge of the business and business person that you are referring because you are putting your brand's stamp of approval on their product/service.

9. **Share your space.** Are you working from an office space? Does it have a conference or training room? If so, consider partnering with businesses that need space for board meetings and/or to host trainings to generate extra income. This not only serves those looking for a space but also helps to promote your

brand because people will naturally want to know more about the business occupying the space.

10. **Get sponsors.** This is tricky because you need a very marketable event or brand to attract the attention of sponsors. I have worked with many clients who are hosting their first event and approaching major corporations for sponsorships. This rarely works unless your personal brand is the draw. Sponsors typically want to see evidence of past results before they invest to determine if the event is a good fit for their brand. After you have hosted an event with some frequency and have collected some data about the attendees, you may be prepared to pitch your event for financial assistance to major brands. Also, be mindful of their process for consideration because some companies only support events that fit within their corporate mission while others have deadlines for receiving and reviewing proposals. Otherwise, consider working with local brands and asking for a reasonable amount of assistance with the goal of your sponsors growing with you.

11. **Become an influencer.** This is often one of the most highly coveted but least easily attainable revenue streams. Becoming an influencer that actually earns income from the brands they promote requires more than having a large social media following. You should have the ability to generate income on behalf of a brand. One of the greatest tests of your brand will be your ability to convince your members to buy/register/join (for a fee). Likes and comments come far easier than dollars. Using your website and social media conversion analytics as a basis for promoting yourself as an influencer in addition to

your social media stats. There are some people who have hundreds of thousands of followers who take action less frequently than people with thousands of followers.

Many people get discouraged when they do not immediately see results from their efforts. There are no get rich quick strategies. Whatever you choose to work on, you need to be prepared to invest time and resources to make it successful. If you are starting from ground zero, it will take at least one year to really get your name out, to find your voice, and to narrow your target market. If you already have an established brand, it may take less time, but you want to be certain that the strategy is adding value to the platform you have established and not serving as a distraction.

LaKesha Womack

LaKesha Womack is the Owner and Lead Consultant with Womack Consulting Group. The firm provides Brand Management, Leadership Training, Strategic Planning, and Political Consulting to clients across the globe through consultations with professionals, not for profit organizations, churches, colleges/universities, and businesses. She has served as a business development presenter for numerous Chambers of Commerce and professional groups. LaKesha specializes in working with newly formed teams, fractured teams, and boards of directors to teach leadership and professional development strategies to enhance communication and improve effectiveness.

LaKesha has a bachelor's degree from Vanderbilt University, is a graduate of the Women's Campaign School at Yale University, and is pursuing a master's degree from Chicago Theological Seminary. She is a member of the Forbes' Coaches Council as a thought leader on leadership topics and contributes to Forbes.com with more than forty business tips provided on their Expert Panel forum.

LaKesha is the published author of ten books and has been featured in numerous publications and interviews providing financial literacy tips, business advice, and community engagement strategies. She has recently launched LaKesha's

Speak Up!

Leadership Circle, a membership platform created to provide personal and professional development resources for individuals seeking to maximize their potential in life.

www.BookLaKesha.com
www.WomackCG.com
www.LaKeshasLeadershipCircle.com
@LaKeshaWomack on all social media platforms

I SPEAK FOR FEE!

HOW TO SET YOUR FEES AND NEGOTIATE VALUE AS A SPEAKER

CHERYL WOOD

Most new, emerging, and aspiring speakers get excited about the idea of being consistently booked for speaking engagements, yet, many become paralyzed at the thought of setting their speaker fee and confidently articulating that fee during conversations with decision makers. In fact, three of the most frequently asked questions by rising professional speakers are:

1. How do I set my speaker fee?

2. How do I know when to increase my speaker fee?

3. How do I position myself to always generate my speaker fee?

UNDENIABLE FACT: The more you speak, the more experience you will gain and the more credibility you will develop, thus, increasing your speaker confidence, the impact of your delivery, the demand for your services, and ultimately, your speaker fee!

Consider the following discussion regarding these top three questions:

1. *How do I set my speaker fee?*

The first step in setting your speaker fee is to adopt a mindset of *worthiness* and *expectation*. You must *expect* to be reasonably compensated for your expertise regardless of whether you are considered a novice or seasoned speaker, and you must believe that you are *worthy* of being compensated based on the value you deliver at every presentation. Remember, what makes you most valuable as a speaker is your transparency in sharing what you have personally learned, experienced, overcome, and mastered.

The next step is to understand that there is no hard rule when it comes to setting your speaker fee. There is no official "speaker fee scale" that you are required to abide by. Setting your speaker fee is much like a domino effect: you start somewhere and the more you speak, the more experience and credibility you will gain and the more people you will impact which will put you in higher demand. The more you remain "in high demand," the more you will be positioned to increase your speaker fee.

Oftentimes, speakers will choose to kick-start their career with a low speaker fee (between $500-$1,000) while they gain experience and develop their unique fingerprint in the speaking industry. Other speakers have started with a more competitive speaker fee of $1,500 or $2,000. Again, there are no written rules on the best starting fee. But there is one core rule: You can start high and negotiate lower, but you cannot start low and negotiate higher. For example, if you want to generate $1,500 from each speaking engagement, you might want to set your speaker fee higher, perhaps at $2,500, leaving adequate room to negotiate with organizations looking to book you. This would give you $1,000 of negotiating room. Think about the last time you went shopping for a vehicle. Undoubtedly, you did not pay the amount that was listed on the sticker for the vehicle. Rather, you negotiated.

With that said, there are a few other things you should consider. I encourage rising professional speakers to consider being booked to speak the same way you would consider being hired for a new position at a company. The first thing a company requires from you is your resume that outlines your level and years of experience, education, skill set, and your professional references. Similarly, organizations that consider booking you to speak will have the same requirement. They will want to explore your resume to determine if you are the best fit for their audience based on your experience, skill set mastery, and professional references. Furthermore, similar to a company hiring a new employee, you would not expect an applicant with 5 years of experience to be hired at the same level of compensation as an applicant with 20 years of experience. So, do not fall into the trap of comparing your speaker fee to the fees of speaker gurus who have paid their dues!

Finally, in setting your speaker fee, remember that your fee does not only include the time it takes to deliver your talk. Your fee also encompasses the time to prepare and practice the talk, any materials you prepare for the talk, the time to travel to the speaking engagement, and additional time spent interacting with attendees before and/or after the event.

You may find the following range of speaker fees used by some organizations helpful as you continue to give thought to your speaker fee:

- Beginner speakers are often considered within a fee range of $500-$2,000.

- Emerging speakers are often considered within a fee range of $2,500-$7,500.

- Seasoned speakers with an established brand and "social proof" are often considered within a fee range of $10,000-$25,000.

- Celebrity speakers and influencers with a large following are often considered within a fee range of $30,000-$100,000.

Every speaker must start somewhere. Do not be afraid of small beginnings. And, likewise, do not be afraid to set a higher speaker fee when it is appropriate based on your growing resume, knowledge, and experience. When I launched my speaking career in 2010 it was challenging for me to command $250 as my speaker fee for a Keynote talk. Fast forward to nine years later, I am now able to command $10k as my speaker fee for a Keynote talk. That transition happened as a result of my ongoing mastery, visibility, credibility, and consistency. The more I spoke, the more I invested in myself, and the more I impacted lives globally, the higher I was able to set my speaker fee.

Whatever speaker fee you set for yourself, OWN IT! Set the fee, then practice saying it out loud at least 10 times every day. It is challenging to confidently articulate a speaker fee that you have never practiced saying. And here is what I can assure you: No one will pay you a speaker fee that you do not even think you are worth! So, remind yourself daily: *Someone is searching for what I know **right now** and is ready to pay me for it **right now**.*

2. How do I know when to increase my speaker fee?

When I started my professional speaker career, I followed one simple rule: "Increase My Fee After Three." Whenever I secured a paid speaking engagement at a set speaker fee at least three times, I would then increase my fee. I also took into consideration the investments I made in my own knowledge base along the way. I spent hundreds of thousands of dollars investing in myself with coaches who were at the top of their speaking game so that I could learn and bring that value back to the audiences I served. I was also sure to reflect my newfound knowledge as a part of my speaker fee.

3. How do I position myself to always get paid my speaker fee?

The conversation about your speaker fee should never be awkward or stressful. When in discussion about being booked to speak, always assume that the organization has a budget to pay you by simply asking: "What is your speaker budget for this event?" The organization will typically respond with one of the following:

- They have an allocated budget that will cover your full speaker fee and agree to pay the fee;

- They are only in a position to offer you an honorarium (a portion of your speaker fee) and you can choose to accept or decline;

- They do <u>not</u> have an allocated speaker budget but can offer you the opportunity to "speak to sell" to their audience

Of course, speakers prefer to be paid their full speaker fee. However, try to think long-term and avoid declining a speaking opportunity simply because it only offers an honorarium or is a "speak to sell" opportunity. There might be decision makers in the audience who can book you and pay your full fee to speak at their organization. Not to mention, oftentimes, you can generate more than your speaker fee via "speak to sell" opportunities. Be sure to implement the Speaker "GAN" Process: *Gather, Ask, and Negotiate* – Gather as much pertinent information about the event as possible; Ask the questions that will determine if the event can be reasonably monetized; and Negotiate deliverables that will create a WIN-WIN scenario for you. Every speaking engagement is a PAID speaking engagement when you are intentional and strategic!

Below is a list of recommendations you can make to help an organization find creative ways to pay your full speaker fee:

- Recommend that the organization increase the cost of attendee ticket prices in order to cover your speaker fee (i.e. 200 attendees x $20/increased ticket fee = $4,000 speaker fee)

- Recommend that the organization enlist a sponsor(s) to cover your speaker fee (i.e. 5 speaker sponsors x $2,000 each = $10,000)

- Recommend that the organization create an opportunity for you to sell your program/package to

their attendees (i.e. 20% of 200 attendees = 40
attendees who purchase your $500 package =
$20,000)

- Recommend that the organization purchase copies of
  your book for everyone in their audience at retail cost
  (i.e. 300 books x $25 = $7,500 - $1,500 to purchase
  the books wholesale = $6,000)

- Recommend that the organization promote a paid
  "VIP Meet and Greet" for attendees to meet you and
  take photos (i.e. 20% of 200 attendees = 40 attendees
  who pay $125 each to participate in the Meet and
  Greet = $5,000)

And, if you must "earn" your fee through a speak to sell
opportunity, always request that the organization cover your
airfare, hotel, and ground transportation separate from your
speaker fee.

The one thing that will unquestionably guarantee that your
speaker fee will continue to increase is to always deliver a
stellar talk that leaves a lasting impression no matter how big
or small the audience and no matter what level of
compensation you receive. At the end of the day, event
organizers want to be the "hero." They want to book a
dynamic speaker who is going to WOW their audience, raise
the caliber of the event, and improve the experience for
attendees. When you consistently over-deliver, you will
always be positioned to get highly booked and highly paid to
speak!

CHERYL WOOD

Cheryl Wood is a world-renowned empowerment speaker, social influencer, best-selling author, and master speaker development coach. She specializes in training new, emerging, and aspiring women speakers the tools and techniques for mastering and monetizing their unique story, core message, and subject matter expertise. She empowers and equips women speakers to boldly enter the marketplace knowing their voice is needed. Wood's message of 'taking big risks, facing your fears, and getting outside of your comfort zone' has taken her as far as South Africa, India, United Kingdom, and The Bahamas to impact the lives of others.

Wood is the Curator and Visionary of SpeakerCon, a first-of-its-kind, premiere convention, and awards gala where professional speakers connect, grow, and celebrate. She also serves as the Publisher and Editor-in-Chief of IMPACT THE WORLD magazine, a digital and print publication she launched in 2018 that spotlights the expertise, accomplishments, and stories of celebrities, influencers, and entrepreneurs who are tenaciously pursuing their big dream.

Wood has been featured on ABC, Radio One, Forbes Magazine, Huffington Post, ESSENCE, Black Enterprise, Good Morning Washington, and numerous other media outlets. She has delivered keynote presentations for a host of reputable organizations including: United States Department of Defense, United States Department of Agriculture, the FBI, The United Nations, Federally Employed Women, National Association of Legal Professionals, Blacks In Government, PR News, Verizon Wireless, and Congressional Black Caucus. She has received numerous awards and recognition for her work including 2018 Global Leader Award (When Women Heal Global Leadership Summit), 2018 Woman of Power Award (Women Leadership Magazine USA), 2017 Woman of the Year Award (Zeta Phi Beta), 2017 International Inspirer Award (Boldly Empowering Entrepreneurs Conference), and 2016 Metropolitan Woman of the Year Award (Metropolitan Business Connection).

www.cherylempowers.com
www.instagram.com/cherylempowers
www.facebook.com/cherylempowers
www.linkedin.com/in/cherylempowers

Management!

In this section, you will learn to create systems and processes to manage and grow your speaking business

OBJECTION!

HOW TO NAVIGATE THE LEGAL LANDSCAPE OF YOUR SPEAKING BUSINESS

REGINALD AND HENNITHER GANT

Congratulations! Either you have decided to become, or you are strongly considering becoming a professional speaker and take this business seriously. Now what? As exciting as this journey may sound, it can also be a little scary for those who are brand new to the business side of speaking. With so many questions and concerns racing through your mind, where do you even begin? The following chapter will share ways to help you navigate through the legal aspects and landscape of your speaking business.

Businesses face a variety of legal issues, but not everyone can afford an attorney for every legal problem. As a business owner and professional speaker, protecting yourself and your speaking business is mandatory. There are a vast amount of resources available that you can depend on to make sure you are doing everything it takes to protect and defend your legal interests, and your business. Black Speakers Network (BSN) has a Platform Partnership, with Reginald and Hennither Gant, who are Silver Members and they proudly offer LegalShield and IDShield to all BSN members.

What is LegalShield and IDShield? In essence, it is smart and simple legal coverage and identity theft protection that gives you direct access to AV-rated attorneys and law firms and licensed private investigators all across the United States and parts of Canada for one low small monthly fee. As a professional speaker, you can protect everything that matters – you, your family, your business, and your personal identity with simple, comprehensive coverage. Imagine having peace of mind and protection in the palm of your hand via two dynamic mobile apps! Having a law firm in your back pocket can be the golden ticket to saving you time, money, energy, and effort as a speaker. If accessibility, affordability, and having direct access to experts in situations where you may not know what to do are important, then these services are for you.

As Speakers, we need the 3 pillars of protection surrounding us at all times:

1. Personal
2. Business
3. Identity Theft Protection

Personal Protection

Before we decided to plant our feet in this speaking industry, we were people first. We were men and women with loved ones. Protecting ourselves and families is still important. Consider obtaining a personal plan to protect yourself, your family, and your dependents from trouble. Plans are available for individuals as well. Advice and consultation are yours as you get to speak directly to your legal team about personal matters and other conditions. Should you need your attorney or law firm to write a letter or make a phone call on your behalf that is not a problem. Your attorney will send an official statement while acting on your behalf. How about personal document review? You can get a professional set of eyes on unlimited documents of up to 15 pages or less. What about obtaining a Standard Will, Health Care Power of Attorney, or Living Will? All of these documents are COMPLIMENTARY to the member and their spouse or significant other as a way of saying thank you for being a member of the network.

Business Protection

Now that you have considered and hopefully protected yourself and your family, you can now focus on protecting and running your speaking business with confidence for a low monthly fee as well. If your business and home address are the same, you can add on protection for your business for as little as $9.95 per month. If your business and home address are different, consider the small business plan for $39 per month. What is covered through the small business plan? The following are just a few examples:

- General Consultation – As a Business Owner, you can talk on the phone with your Provider Law Firm about multiple business matters

- Designated Consultation – You can discuss specific legal issues over the phone ranging from topics such as patents to taxes and more

- Contract & Document Review – This one is huge factor for your speaking business. When accepting speaking engagements, contracts are constantly in play. Be mindful that when you are signing someone else's contracts, that their document will have their best interest at heart. Here is where you can send any documents or contracts to your attorney prior to your signature, to ensure you are equally protected as well. This gives you power as a business owner to level the playing field. Make sure everything is accurate and in writing for clients, employees, and more.

- Debt Collection Assistance – What happens if you rendered services but did not receive payment? Debt Collection Assistance is the most common legal problem facing small businesses and you can protect your business from experiencing this with these services.

- Letters & Phone Calls – You have the ability to have your Attorney execute 20 to 40 calls or letters on your behalf as a small business owner. Would you agree that a phone call or letter from your law firm would yield much different results than a phone call or letter from just you?

- In business, never try to go at legal matters alone. Avoid complications by having a professional team on your side that will fight for you and your best interests.

Identity Theft Protection

Identity theft impacts millions of people each year. Criminals are using a variety of scams and hacks to collect and steal personal information from individuals and businesses.

Recently, the Marriott hotel chain reported its data breach which affected over 500 million records. As a Professional Speaker and Business Owner, what are you going to do to protect not only your personal data but those of your clients and/or partners? With IDShield, dark web, social media monitoring, and credit monitoring are all part of the service. You can choose between obtaining an individual plan or a family plan. Since identity theft is one of America's biggest plagues, the following is some of what you will receive:

- Security Monitoring – Your financial account numbers and lending services are monitored to ensure your information is not used in fraudulent situations

- Privacy Monitoring – Areas in which fraud are often reported are heavily monitored

- Social Media Monitoring – In the age of social media, make sure your reputation and privacy are protected

- Identity Restoration – Should your information become compromised, this service will do everything in their power to restore it back to pre-theft status

- Consultation Services – You can get tips and advice from Licensed Private Investigators plus assistance in emergency situations 24 hours a day, 7 days a week

In addition to the 3 pillars of protection mentioned above, imagine being able to save money at over 400 vendors nationwide that offer you daily discounts. As a business owner, it is not how much money you make, but how much you keep that matters. The services already mentioned above also come with a Members Perks program that saves the average individual/family over $2,400 a year. That is money back in your pockets to reinvest back into your business should you choose to do so.

In closing, as an aspiring, new, or established professional speaker, these tips are meant to provide the fundamentals of building your successful speaking. Navigating the legal landscape, of any business, can be scary and intimidating. However, with the proper resources, experts, and protection in place, you can powerfully move forward in the direction of your dreams. Black Speakers Network proudly offers LegalShield and IDShield because they understand the vital importance of the 3 pillars of protection.

For more information or to enroll today for your peace of mind and protection, please visit the BSN link: Bit.ly/bsnlegal

REGINALD AND HENNITHER GANT

Reginald and Hennither Gant are a husband and wife duo with many dreams to serve and be used by God to their fullest potential.

They both grew up in Baltimore and together they have a beautiful family and four amazing children. They are the reasons why they do what they do.

Reginald and Hennither have authored 5 published books between them and serve as Business Owners, Professional Speakers/Facilitators, and Ministry leaders.

The Gants also own their own HR Company, Career Image Solutions, where they provide services to Career Professionals and Business Owners. They also proudly help individuals, families, and businesses protect what matters most with legal services and identity theft protection by offering LegalShield and IDShield.

www.career-image.com
www.bit.ly/bsnlegal
www.facebook.com/careerimagesolutions
www.linkedin.com/in/career-image-solutions-llc-05320398

PROCESS LEADS TO PROFIT!

HOW TO SET UP BUSINESS SYSTEMS

KRISTA JENNINGS

In this chapter, you will be learning how to set up business systems that will allow your business to become an impactful and profitable brand. I will be completely transparent, setting up processes and systems can be time-consuming, but the long-term return is well worth it.

Throughout this chapter, the focus will be on creating a clear understanding of the processes, as well as providing you with steps to support you with implementation:

1. What are business systems?

2. What are processes?

3. Why do you need them?

4. What if I am just starting out, is it that important?

Process equals consistency. To build a profitable business, you need processes. Think McDonald's.

Processes are detailed, step-by-step sets of directions that allow you to achieve an end goal. For example, setting up an email through your email marketing platform. There are many different platforms you can use to schedule and automate emails to your community.

Regardless of the platform, the steps generally will be the same:

1. Sign in.
2. Create the email in a template.
3. Select the list that you are sending it to (if your email list is segmented).
4. Format the email.
5. Send yourself a test email to see what it will look like to the receiver.
   (Active Campaign will allow you to see what the email looks like without sending it to yourself).
6. Schedule the email for a future time and date or send it immediately.

To successfully build a business you need a process and practices to obtain information and to put the information to use in your business. Documentation is an affirmation of order and allows your business to address specific means rather than a generalized end.

Think franchises. Think McDonald's. Let's unpack this example.

I have had McDonald's in a few countries, China, the United States, Canada, and Jamaica (though no longer on the island). The food is pretty much the same in all these countries. The means to make the food follows the same process to get close to 100% in accuracy with food delivery and standards.

Think about how you can deliver an excellent service for your clients while being consistent and personalizing their experience.

If you are a service-based business, the core of delivering excellent service means knowing what you are doing (even if you are just starting out) and delivering in an efficient manner.

Entrepreneurs frequently ask, should you create processes for everything in your business? No, but ask yourself, is this a task that I will likely outsource? Is this something I will do on a frequent basis?

Prioritize these tasks, as this will ensure you achieve the same results all the time.

Fast forward to a few months from now when you have on-boarded a virtual assistant. Consider all the time you will save by not spending all day teaching every single moving part of your business to your VA. Remember we want to use our time efficiently.

What are some other tasks that you do over and over that need to be consistent?

Note that there will be some exceptions to the rules so be sure to document those exceptions.

If you are just getting started in business, it is important that you start to not only consider the short term but to also plan for the long term. This is paramount in building a brand that is truly packaged for profits.

From my experience consulting with start-ups and growing businesses, they want to continue to grow and while they are generating consistent revenue. However, they fail to have strategies that will allow their business to scale as they grow.

Why?

Because everything is in someone's head, generally the business owner or someone in a project management role. As a result, they end up being the bottleneck in their business. What you do in your business cannot be solely dependent on what you know.

You can avoid this by documenting your processes. The collective document of your processes and procedures is your Operations Manual. As a speaker, it is likely that you have other arms of your business. You may be an author, a coach, a consultant, a mentor or providing some type of product/service. Whatever the other arms of your business, you should be aware of how scalable your processes are if you want to grow.

What are systems? They are a set of connected elements or parts that work together for a complex mechanism to work, i.e. your business.

There are marketing systems, financial systems, administrative/customer service, sales, and fulfilment as well as retention systems. These different elements work together for your business to have an impactful. The key is realizing how they work together and ensuring they work in unison.

Your business will not be able to generate sales if you have not done any marketing. Think of your marketing as a system that includes the different moving parts that make up your brand's ability to connect and engage with your dream clients or customers.

Your business cannot collect money if there are not any financial systems in place. It is crucial that you have solid systems working together to allow your brand to truly have an impact. Profits will not magically fall into your lap. You must be intentional. But I must preface with this, systems will not magically allow you to make money while you sleep. You need to make money while you are awake first. That way you know what works and you can leverage that process to increase profits.

When setting up your business systems, you must put some thought into the processes. Before I work with any client to assist with setting up their business systems, we focus on creating a blueprint. This allows us to work toward an objective in the different areas of their business.

Let me provide an overview of what the most basic blueprint should look like for your marketing system.

1. **The source/ platform that introduces someone to your brand.** This could be through paid platforms such as Facebook/Instagram ads, promoted pins on Pinterest or it could be through borrowed platforms such as being a guest on a podcast, an Instagram takeover or through discovered platforms such as SEO that leads to your site, your videos or social media search, or hashtags.

2. **The opt-in box on your home page/ lead magnet.** This should be easy to consume and gives your targeted audience a quick win. People are far more likely to continue to stay connected and to continue to engage when they have received something true of value that was easy to consume.

3. **The email sequence that follows your lead magnet.** This gives you an opportunity to continue to provide valuable content and information.

4. **An offer.** It is important to know what this is before creating the email sequence. What you are offering, will dictate how many emails are being sent in the sequence as well as the content you will be sharing through the email sequence.

The above steps create the funnel that gives your business permission to sell. Your funnel is a sequence of cohesive messages that leads to enrolment or a sale.

As a speaker, you know that your message needs to address the needs, desires, and wants of your audience. The same applies to your business structure. It is about shifting your mindset from winging it, to being intentional.

So back to systems, so what kind of systems should you have in place?

To get started with building out your marketing systems, you will need platforms such as Active Campaign, Constant Contact, Ontraport, MailChimp, Aweber. Utilizing an email marketing platform allows you to have direct access to your community as you continue to nurture a relationship with them and provide valuable content. Social media provides a great introduction to your audience, but you do not have any ownership of what algorithms can take place on Facebook or Instagram. Marketing platforms ensure you have 100% ownership and access to your community.

For financials, PayPal, Stripe, Square, Authorize.net, Skrill, and 2Checkout provides an opportunity to collect payments. Here is a professional tip, do not use only one platform to collect payment.

It is a good idea to ensure your processes are documented on platforms that allow you to give multiple people access so that you can maintain consistency in your day-to-day business operations. Platforms like process.st, Trello, Asana, and Paymo allow you to manage projects while keeping everything organized, transparent and focused on results.

A business that is orderly demonstrates to your customers that you know what you are doing. There is a difference between working in your business and working on your business. There is a difference between income-generating activities and income-generating opportunities.

What is the difference between working in your business and working on your business? Though both are valuable, it is important that time is invested in working on your business. This is where you have an opportunity to build an impactful and profitable business. Let's break this down more. Working in your business activities are basic administrative tasks such as responding to general emails, gathering tracking analytics, and scheduling emails. On the other hand, when you are working on your business you see the bigger picture. It allows you to take charge of your business and see where there are opportunities for growth and expansion as well as areas where you can explore collaborative opportunities. Working on your business allows you to be visionary and take on a more serious role in your business. It also allows you to be innovative. Innovation is at the heart of every exceptional business because it allows you to consistently stay ahead of trends and new developments in your space.

Look at companies such as McDonald's which we addressed earlier, but also Federal Express, Disney, and even Mrs. Fields cookies. These are all exceptional companies that spend a lot of time, resources and money, on determining how they look. Why? Because it pays to consistently appeal and connect with the general audience that they want to provide a service or product to.

Setting up business systems allows you to quantify the level of impact and exposure your brand has. Let's take a step back and evaluate this for your business because it is important to stay ahead and build a profitable business by tracking your analytics. You will not track everything in your business. If you are unsure about what you should start to track, ask yourself the following questions:

1. Which key results do I need to see on a quarterly basis? (revenue growth, by what percentage?)

2. What does growth look like? (i.e. visibility means growing email list)

3. What kind of experience does my brand deliver on? (think consistency)

Therefore, you need to provide content that is valuable to the person you want to attract in your funnel. Ask, is this easy to consume while delivering on a quick win? Get to the core by asking, where along their journey are your informed customers/clients? Note, if it is not easy to consume, the likelihood of them consuming the content is very low and sets the tone for whether they will buy from you.

As it pertains to working on your business and exploring innovation it is very important that you quantify the level of innovation that you have in your business and the impact that innovation can make. Honestly, quantifying is not being done in most businesses and it is a missed opportunity. Throughout my consulting work with start-ups and thriving businesses, I have seen time and time over again where money is being left on the table. This is partly because business systems are not a priority in the infancy stage of building the business or there are systems set up, but they are not cohesive.

If you would like to avoid leaving money on the table then it is important that you start to develop a systems mindset. The whole point of building a business means that you want to have an impact and connect with a specific and targeted group of people.

Working on your business requires that you do strategic work. Working in your business requires that you focus more time and energy into the tactical work. In many instances, the tactical work can be outsourced to freelancers, virtual assistants, and systems experts.

Strategy is where you, the business owner, needs to invest time and energy. To have a business that is thriving and profitable it is important that you get into the habit of outsourcing some of your tactical work, even if you are on a small budget.

Look at it this way, if you could pay someone $15 per hour to put in five hours this week in your business. How much time would that provide you to focus on more strategic growth?

If you are just starting your business and creating structure, it is important that you get into the habit of outsourcing smaller more time-consuming tasks. Therefore, it is key that you start to create checklists, video tutorials, and screen share demos of your processes.

My recommendation is that you have had at least five clients so that you have a clear understanding of the path to attracting and delivering your product/service. You should be able to answer:

1. How much it is that you are generating in sales per client?

2. How much does it cost you to operate your business on a monthly basis?

3. How much are you putting aside as an investment in the growth of your business?

4. How many subscribers did I attract this month, in comparison to this time last year? (Note, Active Campaign shows this to you). If you are wondering why it is important to track this. Think about how having this can allow you to see analyse your marketing activities and plan for the upcoming year.

Now that you are equipped with the tools to set up your business systems, it is time to put it all into place to build a profitable brand.

KRISTA JENNINGS

Krista Jennings is becoming the most sought-after Business Systems Strategist, in the online business community. She is famous for helping entrepreneurs and small business owners strategize how to increase their profit, without working long hours in their business.

www.kristajennings.com
www.facebook.com/kristagajennings
www.instagram.com/kristaajennings

WHAT YOU DO NOT KNOW CAN HURT YOU!

TAXES AND BOOKKEEPING BASICS FOR NEW SPEAKERS

SHAN-NEL D. SIMMONS, EA

Do you struggle with recording and classifying your transactions as a new speaker? You are not alone. Many new speakers struggle with keeping good records of their financial transactions, are unsure how to properly treat transactions as income and expenses are uncertain how to report those transactions on their tax returns.

This chapter will provide you with an overview of the basics for bookkeeping and taxes for speakers. It will widely cover best practices for maintaining good records as well as provide a general summary of bookkeeping and tax treatments for your speaking engagements.

Bad Records Can Hurt You

Whether you are making six figures or nothing at all as a speaker, you must keep records of what you are earning and what you are spending. Keeping track of what is coming in and what is going out is how you will be able to confidently:

(1) determine your pricing

(2) budget for future engagements

(3) transition from speaking as a side-gig to a full-time career

Above are just a few of the benefits that come with regularly keeping track of your earnings and spending. When you keep track of your money, you will be able to make important decisions like those listed above for the direction and succession of your business venture – and the ability to make those crucial decisions all start with keeping good records.

Your recordkeeping process does not have to be any specific method or even software based. If you want your recordkeeping method to be paper only, you can. If you want to use apps and accounting software, you can. As far as the IRS is concerned, whether you decide to keep only electronic documents, only paper documents, or a combination of both electronic and paper documents, you can maintain your records however you like as long as your recordkeeping method clearly shows your earnings and spending, you are able to retrieve your documents, and your documents are legible.[2]

With that said, one of the best things you can do as a speaker is to get separate accounts for your speaking activities from your personal accounts. That means having a separate checking account, a separate PayPal account, a separate

---

[2] IRC §6001, Regulation §1.6001-1, Revenue Procedure 97-22

credit card account, a separate Cash App – you get the picture.

It is best that you do <u>not</u> use your personal accounts to spend and to accept money for your speaking activities. If you must use your personal funds to pay for speaking expenses, you should either write a check or transfer the funds from your personal account to your speaking account. The same thing if you earn money and you want to pay yourself. You should write a check or transfer funds to yourself from your speaking account to your personal account. Some of the reasons you will benefit from keeping your speaking transactions separate from your personal accounts are:

- You can easily see what is being spent and earned from speaking

- You are treating your speaking activity as a business (even side-gigs are technically startup businesses)

- You save time from not having to separate personal or other activity from your speaking for taxes, for lending, for certifications and licensing, etc.

In addition to keeping personal transactions separate from your speaking transaction, you need to know what kind of records to keep. For speaking income, in addition to bank/credit card statements, some documents you will want to keep are, but not limited to, speaking engagement agreements, emails to support payment agreement, and 1099s if applicable. For speaking expenses, in addition to statements, some bank/credit card documents you will want to keep are, but not limited to, receipts, mileage logs, airfare itinerary, and hotel stay statements.

Now you have a general idea of how to keep track of your income and expenses as speaker. But what exactly are typical sources of income and expenses for a speaker?

Not Knowing Your Income and Expenses Can Hurt You

As a speaker, most people are familiar with speaker income being labeled as a speaking or engagement fee where a speaker receives compensation in the form of money. But speakers can receive income in other forms such as, but not limited to:

(1) *Honorarium*: Another monetary fee that is paid to a speaker for services. Speakers usually receive this form of payment when lecturing or presenting to universities.

(2) *Indirect compensation*: This is when a speaker's travel, accommodations, and other cost are paid for without the speaker having the pay the expenses out-of-pocket first. A speaker will have to recognize it as income even though actual money did not exchange hands.

(3) *Royalties*: When speaker receive payment for their books, printed or digital publications, appearing in a documentary/movie/show, it is usually paid in royalties. Royalty payments can continue to be paid to a speaker for as long as the work is circulating.

(4) *Reimbursements*: This is when the speaker is paid back for expenses the speaker paid out-of-pocket.

These are some of the most common forms of compensation for speakers. You should treat them as payment received for your service, and they are income to you as a speaker.

When it comes to what is considered a typical expense for a speaker, most people immediately think of travel costs. But speakers spend money on more than just airfare and hotel rooms. Some common speaker expenses are, but not limited to:

- Business cards
- One-sheets and other printed materials
- Trade show banners
- Headshots and photo sessions
- Software and website fees
- Continuing education
- Credit card merchant fees
- Microphones and other equipment
- Software and website fees
- Public speaking classes or training
- Sponsorship and vendor fees
- Uber/Lyft (if used)
- Facebook and Instagram ads
- And much more

One thing you must remember when it comes to expenses and income as a speaker is how you treat your transactions for financial purposes will differ sometimes from how you treat them for tax purposes. For financial purposes, you want to keep track of all your income that comes in and all your expenses that go out. What is reportable as taxable income and what is treated as a tax deduction can be a different matter.

Not Knowing Your Taxes Can Hurt You

You now know how to keep good records; and you should understand what income is and what expenses are for a speaker. You now need to know how your income and expenses will be taxed. This portion will be a general review of how a speaker is taxed as a sole proprietorship only.

Whether you are working full time as a speaker, or speaking is your side-gig, you will need to report your speaking activity on your tax return – even if you did not make any money. As a sole proprietorship speaker, your speaking activity will be an additional form to your personal 1040 return and will usually be reported on a schedule C.

Speakers typically receive a form 1099-MISC for any payments received from a single forum that exceed $600. You are supposed to report all income received for your speaking services even if you did not receive a 1099-MISC or if you were paid less than $600 for the engagement.[3] Even

---

[3] IRC §61(a)(1)

if you only earned a single dollar, the tax law says you are to report all income received for your services.

You can deduct any expenses that are ordinary and necessary for your work as a speaker[4] and that are incurred for the purpose of you trying to produce income as a speaker[5]. For example, if it is ordinary for you to pay for webinar software to give virtual speeches to earn money, you can deduct the money you pay for using the software against the income you earn from speaking.

Some tax deductions have special treatments when you claim them on your income tax return. You can only deduct 50% on what you spend for your meals[6]. Also, you are required to maintain records for your airfare and your hotel stays to prove those expenses[7], or else you risk having those deductions disallowed if you are audited.

If your expenses are more than your income, you have a net loss. A net loss will reduce your income from all sources you received money (i.e. wages from W-2 job, interest, etc.) on the front of your 1040 income tax return.

If your income is more than your expenses, you have net income. When you have net income, that amount will be subject to self-employment taxes as a sole proprietorship in addition to income taxes. Half the self-employment taxes will

---

[4] IRC §162(a)
[5] IRC §212(1)
[6] IRC §274(n)
[7] Regulation §1.274-5A

be a deduction to reduce your gross income from all sources on the front of your 1040 return. If you did not have enough withheld during the year, or if you did not make any estimated payments during the year, you may owe taxes when you file when you have net income. To avoid owing, make quarterly estimated tax payments, or meet with a tax professional to develop a game plan to best handle your taxes for your speaking career.

This concludes the overview of bookkeeping and taxes for speakers. If you require more personalized advice, be sure to contact Nel's Tax Help for an advice session. Wishing you all the success as a speaker, and may this chapter help you not get hurt when handling your records and taxes for speaking.

SHAN-NEL D. SIMMONS, EA

 Shan-Nel D. Simmons, EA MBA has helped individuals and businesses get out of tax trouble and stay out of tax trouble nationwide with her tax resolution services and educational workshops. She is the owner and enrolled agent of Nel's Tax Help, LLC, has multiple degrees in accounting, and is a former IRS revenue agent. She is gifted in simplifying complex tax laws and procedures for audiences to follow and enjoy.

www.nelstaxhelp.com (business)
www.shanneldsimmons.com (personal)
www.linkedin.com/in/shanneldsimmons
www.facebook.com/nelstaxhelp

WHAT IS IN THE BRAND BAG?
SPEAKER ESSENTIALS FOR THE STAGE
LAYNA WARE

Yes, they just called your name and it is time to make your way towards the stage. Your heart is racing, but your smile is wide, and you are showing no signs of nervousness. As you make your way, your mouth becomes dry, you are wondering if you changed the batteries in the clicker for your presentation, and now you have realized your lucky pen is at the table you just walked away from. This rarely happens to us speakers, right? When speaking locally or globally, there are items we may forget to bring or prepare. The basic essentials that generally come to mind are extra pens, materials, and please do not forget our product(s) or service(s) to sell. But, before pitching from the stage to anyone about anything there are some things that must be in order so that you maximize the time allotted to you.

Properly preparing for your speaking engagements maximizes your influence and earning potential. How? Glad you asked! Your defined win, after stepping away from the podium, is just as important as your message, which is directly linked to what items you need to set aside for your big day. That's right, **preparation** for the **podium** creates the right atmosphere to gain **profit**. For example, you cannot expect to sell 100 books if your card reader was not packed, right? Your expectations must match your intentional efforts to succeed. If you are at the podium to impact lives, transform mindsets and/or provide awareness; relaxing and making sure minutes before speaking are not moments of panic and/or hypertension. When you are prepared to take on the stage and you have the win in mind, there is no stopping you.

Have you ever considered bringing an SD card for your pictures or even an HDMI cord, just in case? No worries, I did not think about these things until IT happened. "IT" meaning the event when you learned a valuable lesson and it goes on your checklist for improvements. Minimizing the number of these occurrences is critical to your growth as a successful speaker. How can you begin to do this? It could begin when you create your personalized list of preferences necessary for speaking events. Certain companies, such as the *Professional Speakers Concierge Service* recognize there are many forgotten details to consider for your speaking event. This is the very reason they outline, within the initial questionnaire, key preferences such as types of water and speaker-friendly snack favorites so that the minor details are thought of for you. Remember, you only have a set window to make an impression and walk away regarded as the expert who had everything all together. Do not be the person who forgot a steamer for that 'lucky' blazer and your wrinkled jacket becomes more memorable than your knowledge.

Here is a general list of items my team carries in the Brand Bag so that any keynote, panelist, or emcee is fully cared for during their speaking engagement:

1. Mints/Gum

2. SD Card

3. Napkins/Tissue

4. Safety Pins

5. Lint Brush/Roller

6. Batteries

7. Lotion

8. Water Bottles

9. HDMI Cords

10. Steamer

11. Credit Card Reader

12. Flash Drive

13. Portable Phone Charger

14. Cuff Links

15. Extra Jewelry Items

Some of these items seem automatic, but we seem to forget them ALL the time. The majority of speakers, if we are honest, forget important items that are necessary for their event. Every speaker will need different items that are essential to their success and dependent upon the win. There is an advantage in understanding what the defined win is and what items need to be brought to create that reality. For example, if you are planning to sell 100 books at an upcoming event; your card reader, informational card, and 'next step' items should be with you. Your selected items will help you to prepare to achieve the goal you have set for that specific event. In this case, if someone is making a purchase or just wanting to connect with you on Facebook, then create then creating simple ways for follow-up and connection will be an important component to the overall win. On the morning of your event, the last thing you want to concern yourself with is having to inconveniently grab something 'really quick.' Let's be realistic. Yes, you want the audience to feel empowered and engaged to do something. However, you too have to be inspired to ensure that every person knows how to contact you, follow you on social media, and most importantly, how professionally sound you are. Having an anticipatory leadership mindset will always set you apart from other speakers.

Let's jump back into the beginning of this chapter. As you walk up the stairs heading toward the podium you take a deep breath and say a prayer hoping your first words come out as you have practiced a million times. Before exhaling you see water and a mint tucked under the podium area, not visible to the audience. You then smile and feel a tap on your shoulder, it is your concierge with your writing pad and lucky pen you mentioned in your brief questionnaire. Feeling like this is now going to be a home run, you speak into the mic to break the ice while opening your water bottle. While everyone is laughing you take a quick swig of water and proceed with the presentation which includes a properly working clicker. Selling from the stage could not have been easier. After the standing ovation, you are ready to take on the world and build connections for future business.

Having a team who travels with you and understands what it takes to win helps you to succeed at another level. Trying to connect with the audience afterwards, while signing books and ushering the next potential customer can be viewed as overwhelming. Professionally, there is hardly any room for error, especially if you are addressing first-time potential customers, followers, and guests. There is something about being **prepared** at the **podium** to gain maximum **profit**. Yes, you can make six or more figures selling your program or generating leads at your booth because you are well prepared. Do not forget the important details that are important to your bottom line.

Layna Ware

 Layna Ware, M.A. is a certified Speaker Coach, who hails from Southampton, New York (Long Island). She has had a passion to witness the growth and development of influencers who can impact individual lives and inevitably, change the world. She has been a dynamic business partner and motivational speaker with over ten years of experience in diverse business environments with an emphasis in training, leadership development, complex problem solving and strategic planning.

Layna demonstrates strategic influence and has translated business needs into people solutions. This businesswoman is committed to serving professional speakers who are at a level in which excellence is the only option. The Professional Speakers Concierge Service (PSCS), an exclusive service for influencers who undergird their responsibility to be at the podium, prefer to have an ON-DEMAND service without needing a full-time assistant and can solely focus only on their message. As the Founder, Layna provides an experience like no other that will foster the relationship between the speaker(s) and the organization they execute for.

"Transforming Innovative Ideas into Immediate Actions!"

www.ProSpeakerService.com
www.facebook.com/Professional-Speakers-Concierge-Service-741604856217147/
www.instagram.com/layna_speaker_concierge
YouTube: Professional Speakers Concierge Service

AFTERWORD BY LES BROWN

You have something special, you have greatness in you.

Hello, my name is Les Brown. I have been speaking for half of a century. It is hard to believe. And I had absolutely no idea when I started out that I would be able to impact people's lives around the world.

Congratulations on accepting and answering the call on your life to use your voice, your story, and experiences to transform the lives of others. You are a messenger of hope. When there is hope in the future, that gives you power in the present. There are people waiting to hear your voice. You have an energy signature and when you speak, there are people who are in a dark place right now but when they hear your voice, they will come out into the light. When you speak, there are people who are fearful, feeling stressed out, and overwhelmed by the challenges in their lives but when they hear your voice, they will feel empowered, you will ignite their spirit, and give them a vision of themselves beyond their circumstances and mental conditioning. When you speak, there are people who feel they cannot make it any more, but you will give them a reason to live. You are God's instrument, a catalyst of action, a messenger of hope. You are God's tool to make the world a better place.

Horace Mann said, "we should be ashamed to die, until we've made some major contribution to humankind." You have positioned yourself to do just that, once again, you have something special. You have greatness in you. I look forward to seeing you on the path. Continue to use your voice to change the world.

LesBrown.com

BLACK SPEAKERS NETWORK

Black Speakers Network, LLC (BSN) is a speaker development and empowerment company with thousands of members around the world. Our mission is to equip, connect, and inspire the next generation of black professional speakers. We help emerging speakers learn how to start or grow your speaking business through access to quality training, resources, and access to speaking opportunities, all while being supported by a vibrant global community of speakers.

Simply put, BSN is here to help you connect to the audience you are called to serve.

How Do I Get Started?

BSN Silver membership is a monthly subscription program designed for speakers who are ready to take your speaking business to the next level. For a small monthly or annual investment, BSN Silver Membership provides a wide range of benefits to help increase your visibility as a speaker, find and book speaking engagements and gain instant access to services that support your growth as a speaker.

To learn more or upgrade to BSN Silver,
visit www.BlackSpeakersNetwork.com

Speak Up! Your Audience Awaits...

Made in the USA
Middletown, DE
16 August 2024

59288838R00155